Freedom From Snakes!

JENIFER,

MAY THIS RESOURCE BE
A BLESSING IN YOUR
LIFE! IN HIS NAME,

06.12.22

Freedom From Snakes!

How I Found Freedom From
A Lifelong Obsession
With Snakes.

Darryl T. Horn
Author, Writer,
& Speaker

www.darrylhornwrites.com

Copyright © 2021 A.D. Darryl T. Horn

Unless otherwise noted, Scripture quotations are taken from the New King James Version (NKJV). Copyright © 1979, 1980, 1982 by Thomas Nelson, Inc. Used by permission. All rights reserved.

ISBN 10: **1088898874**
ISBN 13: **978-1088898871**
Kindle Direct Publishing

Cover designed exclusively by Darryl T. Horn. Cover photo and both interior graphics (pages 3 and 11) acquired from iStockphoto.com. Fonts utilized are Times New Roman Pro Regular and Cataneo BT Standard Regular; both of which are licensed to Darryl T. Horn by MyFonts.com.

Inquiries or questions may be directed as follows:
Addressee: Mrs. Wynell Horn
Communications Director
Email: darrylhornwritesvp@gmail.com

FFS.MnSVrn:21-3, Wil0.

Disclaimer

This book is provided for entertainment and informational purposes only. It is not in any way to be construed as legal or personal advice, counsel, a diagnosis, direction, or guidance in your situation or that of anyone else with whom you may share any of the contents of this book whether intentionally or unintentionally. Please note that this resource is intended exclusively for personal use only. No other use is authorized. If you, or someone you know, has any mental or emotional battle, deficiency, difficulty, or struggle, please see a licensed counselor or medical professional as soon as possible. Do not depend on any of the information in this book in any way as a method for dealing with your situation or that of another without professional assistance.

The realities documented in this work by the author concerning his individual experiences are shared only for entertainment and informational purposes and are not in any way indicative of what may or may not work in someone else's situation.

Again, please, if you need any assistance or help in any of the aforementioned areas of difficulty, please contact a licensed professional without undue delay.

A Personal Note to You!

Dear Reader,

Salutations! As the author of this very unique book, I want to thank you for your interest and investment in it. I also want to express, at the outset, my sincerest heartfelt encouragement for the fact that you are courageously taking a giant leap of faith. Bravo! I realize that, for a variety of different reasons, there are those who would quickly pass up reading a book that had anything to do with snakes. However, I truly hope that you know beyond any shadow of a doubt that it is not by accident, chance, or coincidence that this valuable resource has come into your hands. You may even feel that this book chose you, so to speak, and not the other way around. If you do have feelings along those lines, I can relate, as I did not choose to write this book. I was *chosen* to write this book. I trust you'll see what I mean as we journey through this book together.

As we progress, you can expect to experience a little humor. But that's not the Message of this book. In your imagination you may "see" a few things that you may consider frightening. That is understandable, but fear is not the Message of this book. As I open up and share some of my most personal struggles, you may relate to one or two as well. If you are "tracking" with me, you know that none of that is the Message of this book either.

The most important content of this book is what I call "spiritual truth". This resource is rich with it, and it begins with a prayer of my heart on the page immediately following this note to you. There may be some readers that wish I had left some of this content out. However, I would not be true to Whom I belong, or who I am in Him, or His Calling on my life in these last days, if I had acquiesced in this matter, either by leaving out spiritually relevant content, or by misrepresenting it in any way.

Therefore, if you would prefer to get right to the substance of this book, and skip the spiritual content in the front matter, then by all means, feel free to move ahead to the Preface, Table of Contents, or the Introduction. Perhaps the spiritual content will have more value for you after you have read my story about how the Serpent dominated most of my life until the Savior finally set me free.

With all my heart, I hope that the great Message of this book, in some small way, touches your heart in a forever way, and that it truly helps you or someone that you may know. I hope that the eternal truths shared in this book helps bring the peace of God in your life, or in the life of "whosoever" else it may benefit. May your journey be blessed indeed!

Darryl T. Horn

PS: Be advised that some of the personal identifying characteristics of certain individuals mentioned in this work were altered for their privacy & protection.

A Prayer of My Heart

Heavenly Father,

Thank you for calling, gifting, and directing me to write this book for the benefit of the Body of Christ. I lay it at Your Feet for the fulfillment of Your plans and purposes in the Earth as You desire. Thank you for helping me to write it, finish it, and finally, to publish it for the advancement of Your Kingdom in these last days.

I hereby freely acknowledge the unfathomable excellency of Your grace, Your mercy, and Your wisdom in providing the "preemptive strike" in the Lion of the Tribe of Judah, Who has forever destroyed the power of darkness. Without Whom I could not have completed this assignment that you have so graciously bestowed upon me.

Most of all, I thank You for the matchless Gift of Your Son Jesus Christ of Nazareth. I can't imagine the magnitude of Your sacrifice in making Him my Sacrifice. And with all that I am I thank You for His sacrifice, for raising Him from the dead, and for the fact that He is now seated at Your Right Hand where He is continually interceding for the saints! I am so excited to be one of those looking for His imminent appearing when the trumpet is finally blown for the "catching away" of all who have been made holy and acceptable in Him by His most precious Blood.

Forever Yours,

Darryl T. Horn
October 21, 2021

Dedication

This humble resource is hereby dedicated, without any reservation whatsoever, to the Lord Jesus Christ, my Savior, my Redeemer, and my Deliverer; to His ongoing earthly Ministry; and to the advancing of His Kingdom on planet Earth in these last days; just as He proclaimed in the New Testament Gospel of Luke, as follows...

"The Spirit of the LORD *is upon Me,*
Because He has anointed Me
To preach the gospel to the poor;
He has sent Me to heal the brokenhearted,
To proclaim liberty to the captives
And recovery of sight to the blind,
To set at liberty those who are oppressed;
To proclaim the acceptable
year of the LORD.*"*
Luke 4:18-19

Names of the Holy One of Israel

The Anointed One
King of Kings and Lord of Lords
The Alpha & Omega
Prince of Peace
Holy & Righteous One

The Messiah
He Who was, Who is, & Who is to come
The Rose of Sharon
The Bright & Morning Star
Light of the World

Great High Priest
Wonderful, Counselor, Mighty God
Lord of Glory
Heir of All Things
The Lamb That Was Slain

Advocate
Bread of Life
Commander
Faithful & True Witness
Gift of God

The Horn of My Salvation
Chief Cornerstone
Risen Savior
The First and The Last
Yeshua

The Lion of the Tribe of Judah

Jesus Christ

The Word of God

"And they overcame him by the
blood of the Lamb and
the word of their testimony;
and they did not love
their lives to the death."
Revelation 12:11

{This page intentionally left blank.}

Worthy of Honor

There is a great discourse found in the Old Testament Book of Proverbs, and it is found in the last chapter of the book. I believe, with all my heart, and experience has clearly shown me that my wife, Wynell, is a shining example of the woman described in this discourse. The discourse is aptly called "The Virtuous Wife", and it begins in verse twelve...

"Who can find a virtuous wife? For her worth is far above rubies. The heart of her husband safely trusts her..."
Proverbs 31:10-11a

In case you may be wondering about it, perhaps it would be prudent for me to answer the question for myself before I go any further. Touché! Well, just so you know, I did! I found a virtuous wife. But if I may be so bold, let me go one step further. I have found that Wynell is way more than just *a* virtuous wife. She is, in my opinion, **the** virtuous wife. If you think about it, *shouldn't* all husbands feel that way about *their* wives? And, yes, she has my absolute unconditional devotion and trust in **faith, hope, & love**.

The very next verse of this discourse is also a very true description of her longtime (over two decades!), powerfully insightful, and extraordinarily caring influence in my life.

"She does him [her husband] good and not evil all the days of her life."
Proverbs 31:12

13

The reason I mention this verse is that Wynell has never, and I mean never, done anything to intentionally hurt me. I can honestly say that during the entire time that I have known her, she has always had my best interests at heart no matter what. Again, she is completely trustworthy.

Now while I could certainly continue this tribute down the list of other virtues in this discourse, I find relevant direction in the verses toward the end of this great passage of Scripture, as follows...

"Her children rise up and call her blessed;
Her husband also, and he praises her:
"Many daughters have done well,
But you excel them all.
"Charm is deceitful and beauty is passing,
But a woman who fears the LORD,
she shall be praised."
Proverbs 31:28-30

A close look at the above verses reveals the importance placed on the husband to bless and praise his wife. And I can't think of a better way to bless her than to speak, or write as it were, a personal word directly to her, a declaration of blessing if you will, in these few pages dedicated to her. My desire is that the blessing of her husband may forever remain before her eyes, and the eyes of all who know and deeply appreciate her.

Declaration of Blessing

My Dearest Wynell,

I am so thankful that God chose you to be my covenant helpmate in these last days. Not only are you yourself a great miracle of God in your own right, but with the only exception being what Jesus did for me at the Cross, you are my most treasured miracle.

I am also thankful that He called us to the wilderness for such a time as this. The work that He has done in us during this Pandemic to make us one voice dedicated only to Him, has been the most blessed season of my life thus far. And we know that the best is yet to come!

I so look forward to sharing eternity with you in the Presence of Almighty God, and His Son Whom we serve. Thank you for being the great woman of God that you are. Thank you for walking in faith and patience as we inherit His promises for us in these last days. And may the deepest desires of your heart for our covenant marriage in Christ come to pass according to His highest plans and purposes in the awesome Name of Jesus Christ our Lord. Amen!

Your Loving Husband,

Darryl

PS: Thank you so much for agreeing at the very last minute to quickly draw, just for this resource, the awesome art on page 54. Your artistic gifting is a deep well of creativity which I truly hope will be a great blessing to the Body of Christ, and the advancing of His Kingdom in these last days. Amen!

dth

Preface

This is my story of how a child unexpectedly became entangled with an infatuation for snakes. The infatuation quickly grew into a fierce, unnatural "love" for these post-dinosaur representatives of the modern natural world. Although snakes were the focus of my infatuation from the beginning, it was not just limited to snakes. Lizards and turtles were highly appreciated as well. Amphibians were tolerated; but did not have anywhere near the attractiveness, or "draw" as it were, that snakes did.

The infatuation ultimately became a lifelong obsessive pursuit that spanned over four decades. Refusing all reasoning to consider much more meaningful career alternatives, working with snakes became the number one career direction of this child very early in life. Herpetology, a not-so-popular branch of the biological sciences, became the choice of study after graduation from high school. Herpetological studies in college led to a childhood "dream" coming true in the securing of employment with a major metropolitan zoo in Texas.

However, the dream turned into a career nightmare one day following an epiphany at work, and this professional herpetologist became completely disillusioned with his poor career choice and became engulfed with depression. (This was not the first time I was "bitten" by Depression.) And although this former snake "wrangler" departed from the professional pursuit of herpetology early in his "career", his deeply held infatuation with snakes did not finally come to an end until decades later...

What caused the final disentanglement between this man burdened down with this ungodly infatuation-turned-obsession and his unholy love of snakes? Can anything be extracted from the story of this boy and his love of snakes that can be of help to others? These are just two of many questions addressed by this very unique resource.

In truth, there were two separate events which finally brought an end to the madness in my life. The first event, an unusual snakebite, dealt with the inclination of the natural man. The second event dealt with the spiritual man, that is, the heart connection. Each event, in its' own way, had a powerful influence in helping this man finally walk in Freedom From Snakes.

Have you ever considered the fact that not all snakes on planet Earth can be seen with your physical eyes? Being that snakes are predatory animals; most are really good at being unseen (camouflaged) until they deliver the "bite". Maybe you've already encountered one of these spiritual snakes and were surprised at its' appearance? Perhaps one (or more) is present in your life right now? And even if there are no obviously recognizable "snakes" active in your life right now, if you live long enough, it is highly probable, make that a certain reality, that you will encounter one in the future. When you do, I deeply hope that you, the reader, will take to heart the Message of this resource, and truly find your own Freedom From Snakes.

Table of Contents

Have you ever known someone who had an infatuation? Did their behavior seem odd, strange, or weird to you? The same questions could be asked regarding an obsession. Either way, the identified behavior has as its' focus an object, be it a person, place, or thing. Maybe the object became the focus in the life of the person suffering with it during their early childhood years (as in my case). Usually by ones' teenage years a person has something, even if it's just one something, that he or she is drawn to, likes a whole lot, or absolutely loves. You and I would probably be hard-pressed to find any socially functioning adult, particularly living in America, that does not have more than one something, good or bad, that has become, on some level, a focal point of their life. Healthy somethings may be one thing; but that is not the focus of this resource. This book is about the somethings that tend to result in negative life experiences for anyone that may be involved, and the life-giving Solution made available at the Cross.

So, how does a child become entangled in the coils of an infatuation with snakes? Could there be a dark purpose behind this infatuation, this unnatural "love" of snakes, which is not readily apparent? If this infatuation, like others that could easily be identified, serves a more sinister purpose, how can this be recognized? How does it evolve into behavior that becomes more and more extreme, and may even be described as bizarre? And if the infatuation serves as some type of detour or distraction in one's life, how is it to be effectively addressed? Can a lifelong pursuit of the wrong thing be remedied?

All these questions, and many others, are the "why" for this book. Maybe you're thinking that you don't have a prob-lem with snakes? You've always hated them, and that's not ever going to change. But before you discard this book, I submit to you that maybe this book does indeed have something in it for you. Snakes are certainly not the only thing with which a person can be infatuated or obsessed. And if nothing positive can be extracted from it for use in your life, perhaps someone you know will one day need the truths shared in this resource. Your heartfelt wise expressions of care for them based on having insightful understanding regarding the issues raised in this book can help you to recognize when they need help, and perhaps what may be done to offer it.

You see, snakes you can see with your physical eyes are one thing. But snakes that can only be seen through spiritual "glasses", as it were, are another whole topic altogether. God does want us to both understand and address what's going on in an always active spiritual realm around us that does have real world impact. He certainly does not want anyone of us to be ignorant (unknowledgeable) about how His enemy works against the true children of God in these last days. We must not be ignorant of, or ill-equipped to recognize, the devices our enemy uses to destroy us.

Understanding in this area is critical for at least two identifiable reasons. And you don't have to take my word for it, as the Holy Scriptures are very clear...

> *"My people are destroyed for*
> *lack of knowledge..."*
> *Hosea 4:6a*

> *"The thief does not come but to steal,*
> *and to kill, and to destroy..."*
> *John 10:10a*

Isn't it interesting that our destruction is one of the primary functions of the enemy? If we ignore this, we ignore it at the peril of our own eternal security, and it may even impact that of our loved ones as well. Therefore, it would behoove us to engage in a limited consideration of spiritual warfare in this Holy Spirit directed resource. This book did not come to your attention by accident or coincidence. If you weren't ready for this, the Architect of Creation would not have seen to it that you are now holding it in your hands (or reading it online). His timing is always perfect, and now is your time to step up into a deeper awareness of the intense warfare always raging around us.

If I may use the familiar metaphor of riding in a vehicle, I encourage you to tighten your seat belt, because this is going to be an unusual but rewarding ride. And in some way both you and I will never be the same. And such a result, among many others, is both a wonderful and worthwhile blessing.

Enjoy!

Darryl

Part One: Infatuation

Definitions:

INFAT'UATE, *v.t.* [L. *infatuo*; *in* and *fatuus*, foolish.]
1. To make foolish; to affect with folly; to weaken the intellectual powers, or to deprive of sound judgment. In general, the word does not signify to deprive absolutely of rational powers and reduce to idiocy, but to deprive of sound judgment, so that a person infatuated acts in certain cases as a fool, or without common discretion and prudence...
2. To prepossess or incline to a person or thing in a manner not justified by prudence or reason; to inspire with an extravagant or foolish passion, too obstinate to be controlled by reason. Men are often infatuated with a love of gaming or sensual pleasure.

INFAT'UATED, *pp.* Affected with folly.

INFATUA'TION, *n.* The act of affecting with folly.

Chapter One

How It All Began

My father was a career military man and served the United States Air Force as an Air Traffic Controller for over thirty years. His "Orders" were the cause of the uprooting and moving of our family many times during my childhood. One of the unique places we lived when I was a child was England. We lived there over five years, returning to the United States when I was ten years old. Because of my dads' work, I can still remember watching military fighter jets training, and I learned to enjoy hearing the roar of jet engines from an early age. (I enjoy hearing B1's out of Dyess today, but for very different reasons...) Of course, air shows were standard fare for a military "brat", so I saw plenty of them while growing up. I also remember watching my dad play Basketball and Fast-Pitch Softball at most of the Air Force bases around England. (The bases that I can still easily remember are Bentwaters, Lakenheath, Mildenhall, Upper Heyford, and the base we ultimately lived on - Woodbridge.) I even had the opportunity to see the original Harlem Globetrotters in London at Wimbledon while we were there! Maybe that is what sparked my interest in Basketball.

When we first moved to England, we lived in a house off-base. It was on a round-about in a town called Ipswich. The first school I remember attending was an English kindergarten, where I had to wear a navy-blue uniform with a diagonally striped blue and gold clip-on tie. Man, I remember really disliking that tie! In fact, to this day I refuse to wear diagonally striped ties and wouldn't be caught alive in one. I didn't like the hat I had to wear to complete the ensemble either. I did enjoy playing soccer, and I even remember winning a trophy or two for my short-lived involvement in that sport. It's very possible that I may have even entertained a youthful fantasy about becoming the next Pele'! And I probably would have continued playing soccer when we moved back to the United States, but soccer was not the rage then in America like it is today. It was not a physical fitness activity that employed leagues which organized events readily available for kids back then.

One of the other activities I enjoyed while living overseas was Cub Scouts. I do remember earning a few participant awards, but the merit activity I remember specifically had to do with First Aid. Scouting was an activity I did continue to enjoy once we moved back to America. Anyway, having started kindergarten in England; there I completed the fourth grade. We moved back to the United States the summer before I started fifth grade. I should note here that the school I attended on Woodbridge Base wanted to promote me from the fourth to the sixth grade. Why didn't this promotion happen? My mother would not agree with it. This is very important, not regarding the promotion, but my mother. If you keep reading, you'll see the importance...

The reason I have gone to some length to share with you about my childhood is that I am attempting to paint a true and balanced backdrop for what would become the first cataclysmic event in my life. It wasn't as if I did not have other notable activities or experiences towards which I could have gravitated. Maybe watching fighter jets train when I was a kid is why I still like watching them today. Maybe seeing the Globetrotters at an early age is why I played basketball for a few years in my youth.

If you were to ask me if our family had pets when I was a kid, the answer is "Yes!" Yes, we did. The most mem-orable pet was a dog named "Chee-Chee". There are two reasons that I mention this dog. First, I want you to know that there were pet options other than snakes. The second

28

reason I mention this dog is that it had everything to do with what I remember as the first absolutely demoralizing memory of my life. It also involved a pet Gerbil. The Gerbil actually belonged to my class at school. The teacher thought it was an innovative idea to send the pet home with a different student every weekend to care for it. It was purely on a voluntary basis, and so I "opted in". When my turn came, I happily took my charge home. I sure wish I knew more about the carnivorous propensities of dogs back then, particularly Chihuahuas.

So, I thought it would be a good idea, while cleaning the little guys' cage, to show our dog what a Gerbil looked like. Well, I put the Gerbil in my hand, and then I lowered it to a level where Chee-Chee could see it. I had never seen our dog move that fast before. It lunged towards the Gerbil and grabbed it out of my hand. As quickly as I could, I smacked our dog on the head to get it to release the Gerbil (don't worry, Chee-Chee was not injured). When the Gerbil fell to the floor, I immediately saw the blood. I watched our class pet convulsively bleed to death on the floor. My little heart was broken. As I can recall, that was the first time I cried that wasn't from some type of physical injury. The rest of that weekend, I mourned that Gerbil. Then when Monday morning finally came, I had to take the cage for our class Gerbil back to school empty and explain to the teacher and my classmates what had happened. I can't explain how or why my heart was engaged, but it was. And it is still a sad memory for me to this day.

However, the experience I remember most vividly when we lived in England happened while my maternal grandparents were visiting us. Our family went to London, and we toured several memorable places. But the place that impacted me the most was the London Zoo. More than anything else, what I experienced at the zoo that day set a course for my life that would not be corrected for decades. I would have been about eight or nine years old at the time. I remember seeing lots of interesting animals as we toured the zoo. I specifically remember seeing a Black Panther for the first time. I remember that it was huge, to me at least, and I was really glad there was a fence between it and me!

As we checked out other exhibits at the zoo, I became very curious about the fact that we kept passing by the Snake House. As I remember the sequence of events, when we passed by it the third time or so, I just had to ask about it. Here is what I remember blurting out to the fearless adults in our party, "How come we aren't going in the Snake House?" More than one of the parental resources on the scene strongly communicated to me that "they" did not want to see any snakes. There might have even been some discussion about why there was a lack of enthusiasm, like or love as it were, for the snakes. It seemed to me that they were really afraid, and I didn't understand why (for more about this universal fear, please see Appendix 1). That notwithstanding, I said that *I did* want to see them, even if nobody else wanted to. I was told that if I wanted to look at the snakes, I would have to go in there by myself. So, guess what happened? I did! I couldn't wait to see what everybody else was so afraid of. And, yes, I went in there by myself.

Once inside, I checked out every animal on display. To this day, with one exception, I could not tell you anything about what all the different types of "herps" that I saw were. (The study of reptiles and amphibians is called Herpetology. And "herps" is an insider term loosely used among herpetologists for these animals.) However, the one snake I vividly remember, and have never forgotten, was a Cobra. There are many species of Cobras, and I don't remember what the species was of the one I saw that day. But I do remember this experience as if it happened yesterday. When

30

I stepped in front of that glassed exhibit cage, something happened that I did not expect. It was an exciting experience for me, yet at the same time it was hypnotic and absolutely unforgettable.

Before I share with you what happened, please allow me to give you some background about animal behavior in professional zoo collections (snakes in particular). You should know that when you visit the "snake house" at most zoos, the snakes you see on display are not the only snakes in the building. Most of the time, there are way more snakes off-display than there are on display. Some of the best "stuff" is in the back. And the only way you get to see these specimens is if you work there, volunteer there, or you get invited on a behind-the-scenes tour. Now there are many reasons for why some animals are selected to be on display, and others are not. Since this is not a course in Herpetology, I'll spare you all the reasons for these decisions. I will simply share the one that is germane to our discussion. Regarding snakes on display, the animal selected must be one that does not easily respond to visual stimulus by persons visiting the zoo. I specify visual stimulus for two reasons. The first is that snakes do not have eyelids. Even when asleep, their eyes are still open. (There is a great spiritual lessen in this fact, and it is something to which Jesus Himself referred. For more about this see Appendix 2.) The second reason is that snakes cannot hear sound. They are overly sensitive to vibration, but they cannot hear. That is why most snake houses have signs warning visitors not to tap on the glass. The snakes cannot hear the tapping, but these animals can most certainly feel it. Any movement by the animal in response to the tapping is primarily a response to the vibrations, and perhaps secondarily, the motion, but not the sound. I said all of that to say this. Snakes selected to be on display are there because all they really do is sit there. They do not move around a lot. And they generally do not respond to visual movement outside the cage. Most of the time, they are simply waiting for that next meal. All of which makes what happened to me that day at the zoo truly beyond extraordinary.

When I stepped in front of the cage displaying a venomous (poisonous) Cobra that day at the London Zoo, the snake clearly and visibly responded to my appearance. Suddenly, it "stood" up, and spread its' "hood". As it looked at me through the cage glass, I was absolutely and unequivocally astounded! I thought it was the greatest thing I had ever seen. To say that I was mesmerized is an understatement. Having been a herpetologist who worked in a professional collection at the Dallas Zoo, I'm telling you that what happened with that Cobra was abnormal. Snakes on display almost "never" respond to visual stimulus like that Cobra did *that day*. You can say what you want, but there was definitely an unnatural presence involved that day, and it was not of God. Over the decades I've run into a few naysayers who try to cast doubt on what happened that day, but the interesting thing is this… They weren't there. Nobody was there but God, me, and the Serpent. There was something of great spiritual significance that happened to me that day, and I assure you that it was not good.

Although I should have felt fear for that Cobra, I didn't. I was completely infatuated. My (former) unnatural love for snakes started right there. After this arguably "mind-warping" event I was never the same. Regarding snakes, I was what today is commonly called "all in". I wanted to learn everything I could about snakes. And before we left the zoo that day, I acquired my first book on snakes. Oddly enough, the title of the book was <u>Reptiles and Amphibians: A Guide to Familiar American Species</u>, as I recall. I read that book like it was life itself. From that point on, my appetite for all things snakes was absolutely insatiable. Anytime, and every time, that I found myself in a bookstore or library, the snake books is where I went first. Everything else paled in comparison. Snake books with words helped me grow in knowledge and understanding. Snake books with pictures helped me learn to recognize both the venomous and non-venomous snakes. And that was just the beginning...

A Book I Still Remember

One of the snake books that I read when I was a kid, which I still remember, was a book by a professional Herpetologist, detailing his work at a metropolitan zoo in New York City. The title was <u>Snakes: The Keeper and The Kept</u>. It spoke of King Cobras, and a captive-born Bull Snake that grew to five feet in eleven months, as I remember. It gave me a view to a world that I had become intensely interested in, and one that I could not wait to experience.

Author Notes

My wife and I have a very unusual phrase for this extremely unhealthy familial environment. Interestingly enough, we poignantly call it

*"**Snakes in the Garden**"*.

Chapter Two

My Very First "Catch"!

In the summer of 1973, my family moved from England to Forbes Air Force Base in Topeka Kansas. I was ten years old at the time, and nearly all of my memories of growing up in the United States of America started here. I was enrolled at Pauline Central Elementary School to begin the fifth grade. Pauline Central is where I first played organized Basketball. Even at that young age, my favorite shot was a fade-away Jump Shot from the corner. The usual result? Nothing but net! Well, maybe not every shot...

Anyway, by this time, I had already built a strong herpetological understanding of snakes in America, which included scientific nomenclature, visual recognition of venomous species, and I had a small grasp on variations in venom properties and venom delivery systems of distinct types of American poisonous snakes. All I'm saying is that I knew way more about snakes than the average adult, and I was supremely confident in my knowledge (emphasis on supreme). My ability to truly tell the difference between poisonous and non-poisonous snakes was very soon to be put to the test.

Amongst my new friends in Topeka, I was always willing to share my uniquely vast knowledge about snakes. Soon, I became so glad that I did. One beautiful sunny day while playing with some of my new neighborhood friends, one kid came running up the street looking for me. After confirming my interest in snakes, it was reported to me that there was a snake laying in the front yard of a house just down the street. I want you to know that I did not have to hear that report twice. It might as well have been the Olympic trials because I was off like a shot! When I say I ran down the street to see that snake, you don't even understand. This was a dream come true, and I was not about to miss it.

Once I arrived at the yard (and turned off my military "afterburners"!), I could hardly believe my eyes! There lying in the grass was the most beautiful snake I had ever seen. I still remember it like it was yesterday. It was an absolutely beautiful four- to -five feet long Bull Snake. (The scientific name is *Pituophis melanoleucus sayi*. And no, I did not have to look it up. It is still "burned" into my memory.) Do you remember me saying earlier that I was "all in"? What lay before me is what you might call a pop quiz. I still remember a question circulating in my mind regarding whether I was just going to stand there and look at it, or if I was actually going to capture it? What do you think I did? What do you hope I did? Man, I grabbed that snake like it stole something! Don't worry, I did use the proper herpetological technique of grasping it firmly behind the head with one hand and supporting its' body with my other hand. Right then I made that snake <u>mine</u>! Or so I thought. Little did I know that all kinds of drama in the 'hood was about to begin...

Now you would think that my mother would be so proud that her firstborn son mastered the art of catching snakes at such an early age, right? (My dad was at work, and mom was the parental resource that was home at the time.) If you said "No", you're right! Although I did have a firm grasp on that snake, apparently I did not have a firm grasp on reality. The reaction of my mother, who watched me walk into our yard holding a large snake, which was now fully awake and quite displeased with having had his afternoon delight nap interrupted by yours truly, was nothing less than infamous. She was in our kitchen talking on the telephone to one of her friends, when she looked out the kitchen window, and saw me holding what was obviously a very real snake. She could tell because of how vigorously it was now wiggling in my hands. (And just in case you are wondering, the snake itself was not "all in" with being handled!) My mother dropped the phone, and then she ran her Olympic trial-qualifying run out of our house and into our front yard where I was proudly standing with my trophy.

When my mother cleared the garage, she issued clear, direct, and awfully specific high-level communication. What she yelled was unmistakable, "Drop that snake!" However, I was neither moved, nor dismayed. Here I had the "catch" of the century, my dream, my first snake, and she wanted me to drop it? Are you serious? I attempted a strong rebuttal with "But mom…" I did not even have a chance to stand my ground for my dream that was finally realized. My rebuttal was interrupted with the standard parental resource override, "I said drop it now!" Her verbal command also carried with it significant parental undertones, verbal nuances which clearly indicated that the trouble I was in might potentially be terminal, and not at all survivable, depending on how much mercy may or may not be available in response to my incredibly dastardly deed.

What's a kid to do? I had no choice other than to obey what I was told to do. I dropped my prize, my dream, my catch of a lifetime, right there in the front yard of our house. The next insane instruction from my mother was even more astounding. She said, "Go take a shower." Well, I was not at all finished with the debate, so I responded by saying, "What?" My prize then was to get that instruction a second time as well. Of course, I obeyed that command too. What choice did I have? I look back now, and I still do not understand why I had to take a shower. If the snake had been venomous, and had actually bitten me, just what was a shower going to do? (Having been a professional, I'll just tell you that a shower would have done nothing in this case if I had indeed been bitten by a venomous snake. In truth, it would most likely have made things much worse.) I am quite certain her direction was one of those "get-that-knucklehead son of mine out of the way", so she could assume command of my "crime scene" …

Nevertheless, I completed my assigned task as quickly as I could, because I was very concerned about what would happen to "my" snake. When I finally made it back to the front yard, the scene that had developed was absolutely unbelievable. My mother pulled out all the stops to have this situation addressed and resolved to her satisfaction (emphasis on her). She wore that telephone out calling people to come get "my" snake. Since we lived in base housing, she started with the Military Police. When they arrived, they took one look at that snake, and reported to her that there was nothing they could do with it, so they were not touching it. She called the Fire Department. She called the Topeka Police Department. She even called the "Dog Catcher." All these first responders were standing around my front yard, all afraid to have anything to do with "my" snake. If there had been cell phones back in the day, I am quite certain it would have gone viral. Between all the first responders, neighbors, and my kid friends, there were 25-30 people standing around in our front yard all because of a harmless Bull Snake!

The call that was definitely the "gamechanger", was the call my mother made to the Topeka Zoo. I do not know who she harangued into responding to our situation, but the Zoo sent a herpetologist out to our house to get the snake. (Later in life, during the time I worked at the Dallas Zoo, I never made a "house call." We did not have time for that!) I do not remember who the person was that responded, but he or she was the hero that day in Topeka Kansas. "My" snake was captured without incident. Some weeks or months later when we visited the Topeka Zoo, I looked for and saw what I believe was "my" snake on display in the snake house. It may not have been, but at ten years old, it looked like it to me. I am sad to say that I had significant emotional attachment to that snake because of the buildup to it being my first catch. I assure you that it was not my last, as my infatuation only grew stronger. I enjoyed other really cool herpetological adventures during the two years I lived in Kansas, but my first catch was the most memorable.

There is one other adventure worth sharing as my memory of it is still vivid, and it had to do with my continued enjoyment of Scouting. By this time, I was now a "Webelo", and was finally old enough to participate in camping. I do not remember where we were on this campout, but I just knew I had made a never-seen-before new herpetological discovery. Please let me preempt my story with an honest acknowledgement that, as I said in chapter one, I did like some lizards, but I could not be described as "all in" where these reptiles are concerned. Consequently, I spent very little time studying lizards, pictures of them, or their scientific nomenclature.

So, after we set up our campsite, and as soon as I had some free time, my hunt for snakes began. Being that snakes tend to really be secretive predators, hunting for snakes is not a passive sit-and-wait activity; you really do have to actively go looking for them. And if you don't see any that happen to be out in the open, peeking where the creature may be hiding is the next best thing. Turning over logs, rocks, or sheets of what-have-you is quite often remarkably effective in finding the prize. That day, turning over rocks was how I made my great discovery.

As I excitedly engaged the hunt, I do not remember how many rocks I turned over, but when I saw that first lizard, my surprise and excitement registered on the Richter Scale, I'm sure. This lizard was about nine or ten inches long, had a broad muscular-looking head, and had this strange, speckled design making up the pattern of the scales. Now, even though I did not recognize it at all, I did know that it was not dangerous to me. I had read enough about lizards to know that it was neither a Gila Monster nor a Mexican Beaded Lizard. I would have easily recognized those two dinosaurs. So, as soon as I knew it was not dangerous, I grabbed that joker before it could even think about escaping. I caught two more just like the first on that same campout, and in my pre-teenage brain, I thought I was a herpetologist extraordinaire because of what I thought I had discovered. And yes, I was completely deflated and dejected when I found the picture of that very same lizard already in the books clearly identified as a Great Plains Skink. I guess I arrived on the herpetological scene a few decades too late to be a pioneer in that field. Que sera sera!

If you are wondering if I encountered any snakes on that particular campout, I do remember playing around with a non-venomous Blue Racer. It was a small snake (two and a half to three feet long), but it was a snake no less. I certainly enjoyed my brief encounter with it, and I did not take it home. In fact, I do not remember what I did with that snake; I am sure I released it somewhere near the campsite, but I don't remember for sure. My memories of it are not as vivid in light of my great "discovery" of the undiscovered Skink, coupled with my joyful anticipation of sharing my discovery with the herpetological world. How sad is that?

As I can best recall, it was around this time in my life when those around me started asking me questions regarding my future occupation. I would frequently be asked, "What do you want to do when you grow up?" Perhaps I was asked this question so much, because the source of the question was hoping that my infatuation with snakes was just a pastime, and that it really was not going to be my career choice. It is popularly said that "hindsight is 20/20". That certainly is true in this case. To my regret, those who asked me that question were often very disappointed. For the most part, my answer was always, "When I grow up, I want a job working with snakes!" Nothing else was even on my radar. As I look back, there are many reasons my whole pre-occupation with snakes was regretful. As far as I am concerned, there is only one positive reason my regretful fantasy was "allowed" to direct my life during the formative years of my childhood, beginning from that cataclysmic day at the London Zoo. My infatuation brought me to Texas; not for my life then, but for the life that God has called me to and prepared me for now in my latter years.

Part Two: Obsession

Definitions:

OBSESS', v.t. [L. *obsideo, obsessus*; *ob* and *sedeo*, to sit.] To besiege.

OBSESS'ION, n. [L. *obsessio*.] The act of besieging; the first attack of Satan antecedent to possession.

LICEN'TIOUS, a. [L. *licentiosus*.] Using license; indulging freedom to excess; unrestrained by law or morality; loose; dissolute; as a *licentious* man.

2. Exceeding the limits of law or propriety; wanton; unrestrained; as *licentious* desires. *Licentious* thoughts precede *licentious* conduct.

LICEN'TIOUSNESS, n. Excessive indulgence of liberty; contempt of the just restraints of law, morality, and decorum. The *licentiousness* of authors is justly condemned; the *licentiousness* of the press is punishable by law.

> Law is the god of wise men;
> *licentiousness* is the god of fools.
> *Plato.*

Chapter Three

Snakes In The South

In the summer of 1975, my dad got USAF "Orders" to go to Korea. His assignment was to be TDY (a military acronym which stands for Temporary Duty Yonder) and would last up to around a year. Families are not allowed to participate in these moves for distinct reasons, so we moved from Kansas to Alabama, settling in a tiny suburb of Mobile called Eight Mile. I was enrolled in a school called Sidney Phillips Middle School in preparation for beginning my seventh year of public school. Having taken percussion lessons in the fifth and sixth grade, I was able to participate in the concert band at school. But as had happened previously in Kansas, I had to make new friends, and my new friends quickly discovered that I was different because I "loved" snakes. In fact, more than a few of my new friends affectionately referred to me as "Snake". My other nickname this particular year was "Bigfoot". As I recall, it may have had something to do with my size thirteen (13) clodhoppers! It was during my time in Mobile that my infatuation with snakes truly grew by leaps and bounds, now morphing into a whole new level - obsession.

One day at school, I, along with some of my friends were enjoying recess. We were playing outside, and along with the standard "jungle gym" equipment available for our use, there was also a field (for track) available for our escape-from-the-classroom festivities. I don't remember if I was the first one to spot the snake in the field, or if it was someone else, but as soon as I was in proximity to this speedy little beastie, the chase was on! What I saw is called a Black Racer. It is non-venomous, and it was diligently living out its' name trying to get into a hole in the ground. His escape attempt was absolutely unacceptable to me, and I was not going to be denied the capture of my feisty new "friend". So, I was forced to resort to my "superman" dive to catch this spectacular specimen, and I got it! The three-foot snake had only made it about halfway down the hole, so I was able to gently pull my new capture back out of that hole, and my herpetological "joy" was renewed with this new reptilian acquisition!

I was able to take this one home, but I'm sure you already know the answer to the question you would have to be wondering. Did I make my mom aware of my new catch? The answer is "Absolutely not!" And this capture would not be the last reptile I would sneak into the house. My infatuation now-turned-obsession was not about to be squelched by mere parental fear or any other negative repercussions. Even my little brother, Eddie, became an accessory to my herpetological pursuits, and our most famous hunt happened outside of a bowling alley in Mobile.

My mom had joined a bowling league, and Eddie and I were unambiguously instructed to stay inside the venue chosen for *her* entertainment. And just so you know, neither of us had any misunderstanding regarding her instructions. However, the "call" of what we might find outside in the creek soon drowned out her parental directives. As soon as she became fully engaged in her game and was no longer giving us the frequently familiar parental stare-down (some people call it a "mean-mug"), we made a run for the doors. Bursting outside of our boring enclosure, we gleefully headed straight for the creek. Do you think we gave any consideration to the dangers of what we were doing? The answer, of course, is "No." I was all about the chase of the find, and catching it, no matter who it endangered. Endangering myself was one thing. But that did not give me the right to endanger my little brother. That was insanity.

46

That last sentence is why I now know that what I was doing **is** called an obsession and is not anywhere in the arena of normal. There were more than a few dangers outside the watchful eye of my mother. There was a very real possibility of drowning or incurring other types of injuries. And what if we had run across a venomous snake and either of us had been bitten? It's not like I had us out there with a first aid kit and anti-venom. We didn't have a cell phone to dial 9-1-1 for help. Hello! This was 1975! News for you! There weren't no cell phones! (I know that is bad English, but ya'll will just have to forgive me for that one.) Either of us could have easily lost our lives down in that creek, but God...

So, what did happen in that creek outside the bowling alley? It was another "catch" of a lifetime. As we walked along the edge of that creek, we spotted an enormous Common Snapping Turtle. (I have not provided the scientific name for this guy, because I was not into the Latin names of turtles; I was only interested in snakes.) Having had some experience with these present-day leftovers from the era of the dinosaurs in Kansas, I knew by the size of this critter that it was anything but common. I just had to have it. My little brother and I quickly developed a plan to capture "Mr. Snapper". Our plan called for us to physically get into the creek, which was at least waist deep (I'm sure deeper in some places), and we had to coordinate our movements in the water to effect the arrest, I'm sorry, to affect the capture of this pre-historic denizen in the creek. As I can best recall, it took what seemed like about an hour for us to finally extract it from the water, and what a glorious moment that was! Our plan worked, and we were overwhelmingly successful in executing our mission! But now we had another more complex problem. What do we do with it?

I know there are some folks in the South who would have made themselves some turtle soup. I had absolutely no interest in that, and neither did my brother. I simply wanted to enjoy the uniqueness of this great creature for just a little while. So, we went about the task of finding a suitable container to hold our Behemoth, so that we could take it home. Once we found a box, we secretly concealed the box under a seat in our family car (affectionately known as Big Blue), and we went back into the bowling alley doing our best to look quite innocent, as I recall. If mom noticed anything different about our clothing from our excursion, she did not say a word all the way home. Unfortunately, the trip home was not anything like I thought it was going to be.

Both my brother and I sat on the middle seat of our station-wagon to monitor the condition of our prize, and to make sure it was secure. We were in for a surprise. Little did we know that this turtle had covert next-level escape skills, and it got out of the box! When I determined that the turtle was out of the box, this is what I said to my brother as quietly and urgently as I could, "Eddie, the turtle got out! Pick your feet up; he'll bite you." We rode all the way home holding our feet up, and I was really hoping (praying?) it did not bite mom who was navigating us to our domicile. Of course, we did not inform her of our catch or of the fact that Mister Turtle had escaped his temporary enclosure. That would have been catastrophic; maybe not for Mr. Snapper, but most definitely for us!

Looking back now, it should have been clearly obvious to mom that we were up to something when we parked at our house, and my brother and I stayed in the car. Normally we couldn't wait to get in the house to eat, but not this time. We had a job to do. We had to locate our escapee, re-capture it, and then we had to figure out where to secure it overnight until we could decide what to do with it the next day. To be honest, finding the turtle was easy. It's not like it opened the door, jumped out, and deployed its' parachute to soften its' landing on the open road. It had to still be in the car, and I am so thankful it was! We found it, captured it, and put water in a large trashcan to help the little guy with hydration during the night. The next day we decided to let it go in a nearby creek. To our amazement (and we were glad of it), mom never knew about our escapade with the turtle until well after we were grown. While our hunt and capture of that turtle makes an exceptional story, it's only a very small part of the picture of how I continued to grow in herpetological understanding and experience while I lived in the South. I should probably point out that the next time my mom joined a bowling league while we lived there, she made sure that I was on the team. Can you see any wisdom in that? If you think about it, if I were bowling, I could not be outside hunting for snakes. Smart move! While participating in that league, I once remember bowling a 179. I do not think I have ever again come close to that score since.

Once when we were visiting some cousins in Pritchard (just down the road from Eight Mile), after the initial "Hey ya'll", I became bored with all the general conversation, and the call of the outside got all over me. I just had to go investigate what looked like a forest across the street. As I crossed and walked off the road, I realized that there was a sizeable stream, which I was not willing to cross to get to the woods. As I stood there thinking over my dilemma, I noticed something moving on the bank on the other side. What I saw was a very large Mud Snake! This was the only time I ever saw one in the wild. And I have seen very few in captivity, as these particular snakes are exceedingly difficult to keep in captivity because of the specialized prey that is necessary for their consumption (Amphiumids, Frogs, and Salamanders).

While out playing with some friends of mine in Eight Mile, I caught my first King Snake. It was a sizeable Speckled King Snake to be exact (*Lampropeltis getulus holbrooki*). King Snakes were definitely one of my favorite snakes, and for certain environmental reasons, they still are. Besides having a ravenous appetite for small rodent-type critters that regularly "squeak", they kill and eat (by constriction) other snakes, particularly venomous ones like Rattlesnakes, Water Moccasins, and Copperheads. If you own land, you should be grateful to have king snakes about your property. They are not venomous, are not normally aggressive towards people, and they generally try to avoid human contact. Even if you run across one in your yard in the city, you would still be wise to let them be. Think of them as "friendly" snakes. Although they do make great pets, I no longer promote the captive keeping of snakes as pets. Not anymore.

For those who may be wondering about our family dog, Chee-Chee, let me get back to it. I really had not yet learned the lesson that Chee-Chee, like you and me, had times it was not interested in playing. It was now time for me to learn this lesson in a more personal way (go ahead dummy!). One day I put Chee-Chee up on a coffee table, and the name of the game was, "Growl in Yo' Face". Still not understanding just how quick she could be, I growled in her face one time too many. The unmistakable scar on my upper lip concealed by my mustache tells the rest of the story… Sadly, Chee-Chee was killed by a car after she had run into the street in front of our house. I was playing Baseball at the time and didn't find out till I arrived home. Nobody even had the guts to tell me about it (especially before I got home). I remember sitting at the dinner table, and my siblings were unusually quiet, as was my mother. All of a sudden, I realized that I had not seen our dog. I blurted out, "Where's Chee-Chee?" And that's when my mother told me what had happened. That was the fastest I had ever run from the table to my room, because the damn broke, and my tears flowed. So, you see, I genuinely cared about Chi-Chi.

It is probably important for me to introduce a new family activity that occurred with some regularity while we lived in the South. I do not remember our family engaging in much of this particular activity before (if at all) or afterwards. It was something we engaged in only while we lived in the South. It had to do with attending a church, and it was all very new to me.

To be honest, when our family (minus my dad) started attending Friendship Primitive Baptist Church on St. Stephens Road in Pritchard, I found it somewhat interesting, but it was not one of my favorite things to do. In fact, one day my brother and I were informed that we were going to be baptized. I had no clue what that was about, but I knew that it would have been futile to resist.

You see, my maternal grandmother, who, believe it or not, everyone, including my brother and I, called "Big Mama", was a most interesting lady. She drove a big 1970's 4-door Cadillac, and yes, she carried a handgun in her purse. I actually saw her pull that gun out of her purse when we were stopped at an intersection one day, and a Klansman (KKK) who was collecting donations had the gall to approach our car. Big Mama didn't play! Oh, did I tell you that she was a Deaconess at the church? If you have never lived in the deep South, you have never seen the devils of Racism like she did. That was over forty, that's four-zero (40), years ago, and Racism is *still* as devilish and evil today in this country as it was back then, if not more so… (Thank you former President. What a clown!)

Grand Walter, my step-grandfather, was the husband of Big Mama, and he was also one of the Elders of that same church. He was an inspirational preacher, as I recall, and also a very industrious man. I always had nothing but respect for him. Both Grand Walter and Big Mama have gone on to Glory, and I still treasure their memory.

Anyway, getting back to my brother and me, we were water-baptized in the church baptistry, but I didn't feel any different afterwards than before I was "buried". I certainly lacked even a little understanding about this practice, but I also lacked clear teaching about it from the Word of God. Sometime after that, my brother and I were "at it", as was our custom, and Big Mama said, "You 'sposed to be different." That was news to me! And for a long time after that, it was also a conundrum. I have much understanding about water baptism today, as later in life I chose to be baptized based on **my** faith.

Let me now change "gears" and share with you the last important herpetological facet of my adventures in the South. One day while riding in our car, I spotted a pet shop (Aquarius Pets on Springhill Avenue), not far from where I went to school. I just had to see if they had any snakes there. (Anytime I was anywhere that had unusual animals, I always looked for snakes.) To my incredulous surprise, they had more than a few snakes in that pet shop. Most of them were for sale (for pets?), but a few were not. It didn't matter to me, because I was just happy to see a collection of snakes. I asked the owners if I could help clean the cages, and so began my first experience in volunteerism. Although they did have a few venomous snakes, I was specifically instructed not to open any of those cages. I happily complied with that command because I clearly understood that they were dangerous. I definitely did not want to get bitten by one of those creatures. And at that time, I was not into taking risks involving animals with lethal capability. Of course, as my obsession deepened, that too changed. As I recall, the pet shop did not have anti-venom immediately available either (that I knew of). That is a realm of insanity on another level.

But at that time, I did not care. I simply enjoyed cleaning the cages, handling the snakes that I could, and I even got to feed some of them. To me, observing a snake eat its' prey was one of my favorite things to watch. I never got bored with that most unusual aspect of Herpetology.

My favorite snake in that collection was an Eastern Indigo Snake (*Drymarchon corais couperi*). I had never seen one before, and I really enjoyed "handling" that particular snake. It was large, over six feet as I recall, and was never aggressive towards me while being handled. In fact, it was the only snake I ever heard "hissing" as a matter of course, as it gently crawled around my neck close to my ears. That was always exciting to me! I found a new friend!

During this one year in Mobile, I grew tremendously in my understanding based on all the experiences I had there. However, the time came to move again, so I had to say goodbye to my new friends again, and my time working at the pet shop ended, much to my fairly deep disappointment. But military life being what it was, this young man went West when my dad got his new orders. Although it saddened me to leave Mobile, I was looking forward to being back in a region where there was again the very real possibility of catching big boisterous Bull Snakes.

The creator of this drawing is my beloved covenant wife, Mrs. Wynell Horn. More than just a great drawing to me, it is a reminder of a horrible event, which occurred while living in Wichita Falls. On April 10, 1979, I was watching a movie called "The Promise" at Sikes Center Mall when an employee of the theatre warned us that there was a tornado on the parking lot! Categorized as an F5 at that time (before the Enhanced Fujita Scale), the tornado was reported to be half a mile wide on the ground. Loss of life was tragic, and the damage caused, well... I have never forgotten that day. Today, every time I hear news of a tornado, and the tragic loss of life and property it causes, I remember...

Chapter Four

Snakes In High Schools

There is a reason that "Schools" in the title of this chapter is plural. The reason has everything to do with the very important obligations of my dad to the USAF. After he returned from Korea, his new Orders required our family to move to Shephard Air Force Base in Wichita Falls, Texas. I finished the seventh grade in Mobile, and then headed west with my family to start the next chapter in the unfolding of my adventures through this life.

Wichita Falls, Texas

Life in the town of Wichita Falls offered me a variety of different experiences once I was able to acclimate to the incredible heat. When we moved to this midwestern town situated almost perfectly in what is commonly known around meteorological circles as Tornado Alley, it was August, about three weeks before school was to start. Since I mentioned the incredible heat, can you guess why Wichita Falls played host to the annual "Hotter N' Hell 100" Bike Race? (At least it did before the worldwide onset of the COVID-19 Pandemic.) I am quite certain it has something to do with how incredibly hot it typically gets in August. Talk about frying eggs on the sidewalk!

I was now preparing to enter the eighth grade, and I, along with all the other military kids on base in seventh and eighth grade, rode a "Yellowhammer" (a school bus) to a school called Northwest Junior High School (it is now called Kirby Middle School). Other budding "hobbies" were now calling for more and more of my time and attention. I continued my joyful involvement in Band, but now participated in marching band as well as concert band. I returned to playing scholastic Basketball that year, and also participated in Track and Field. I played Baseball in an on-base youth league. I confess, I certainly did enjoy pursuing all those extra-curricular activities if only for a season.

One of my longest-lasting pursuits, which developed in this season, was a deep appreciation and practice of Martial Arts like my father before me. Although at that time I was only interested in certain aspects of it (sparring primarily), my training in this area on the base included a type of Korean Karate called Tang Soo Do. I regret to say that I did become a fan of Bruce Lee, and I saw his last movie "Game of Death" three times at a theatre (on the base as well). I also remember seeing the movies Rocky, Star Trek, Superman, and a movie called Street Fighter on the base as well. Needless to say, there was a lot of very unrealistic stuff entertaining my impressionable teenage mind at that time. I really did not acquire much in the way of experience with snakes during this time in my life, but I did continue growing in knowledge.

There was one very memorable event involving a snake, which happened to me while living in Wichita Falls. It would have to have occurred during my eighth or ninth grade year, because my dad got orders back to Korea when I was in the tenth grade; so, this event could not have happened while he was again TDY. We took a family picnic to a state park called Lake Arrowhead. It was just a day outing, and it was exciting to me because it was some place new to me. Some close friends of my parents came with us, and we enjoyed a nice luncheon in the park. As was usually the case, my parents began engaging in some interesting conversation with their friends, to which I always enjoyed listening. However, it was not too long into their social discourse, before my dad told me, "Go find a snake." I am certain that neither of my parents really thought that I would. But that was not the best assumption to make, nor the best direction to give to a teenager who, by then, had been obsessed with snakes for seven or eight years. In fact, it was almost like a straight up challenge (to me anyway), and I was definitely up to the task. So off I went!

I am not certain how long I had been walking a long way off the pavement (in the grass) when it finally happened. I had wondered for years what it would feel like when I found "my" first venomous snake, and now here it was right in front of me. (Notice that I was looking for a "feeling".) This was my first contact with a wild, un-caged Rattlesnake (I will not bore you with the Latin name this time). To be specific, it was a Prairie Rattlesnake, and it was only about 2 and 1/2 feet long. I certainly was not expecting to find a venomous snake. My hope, as usual, was to find a big Bull Snake, but this "find" was exciting enough! There was one drawback though. I had sense enough to know not to try to "handle" it without the proper equipment. I say sense, because when you see people "free-handling" venomous snakes on the various online viewing platforms that are so popular today, true herpetological professionals who do not engage in that kind of reckless behavior, regard it as absolute narcissistic foolishness, and I certainly concur. In fact, the danger factor is another aspect of obsessive (compulsive?) behavior, and it should always be viewed as a "red flag".

Anyway, when I saw the venomous beastie, which I was walking right towards, I stopped in my tracks. Yes, it did rattle, but if I had been twenty feet or more away when it did, I may not have even heard it. When you hear a rattlesnake rattle, you should always try to first visually locate where it is *before* you take off running. Because if you run the wrong way, you may end up stepping right on it. That, of course, would be a huge mistake, and it would most likely be a very painful one. (That is, unless you have received what is called a "dry" bite. Please see Appendix 1 for more about this unusual phenomenon.) So, once I visually acquired its' position, I slowly backed out of striking range, moving myself further away from any potential injury.

I then did what any other caring conscientious teenage boy would do, after being told go to find a snake. I called out to my dad and said, "Dad! I found one!" What do you think was his response? Do you think he came out in the grass where I was to see my prize or help me catch it? If you said "No", once again, you are so right! He stood up from the picnic table, walked to the edge of the grass, and from a distance began throwing nails at the snake, which he could not possibly see, because he was too far away. I am not quite sure why he had nails on-hand to throw, but that is beside the point. He then immediately instructed me to get out of the grass, which I did without even attempting to stand my ground with him, because he was dad. Dad was large and in charge. Only a fool would have attempted to challenge him, and I was not the one, neither that day nor any other. So instead, I had to settle for just seeing one, but without being able to touch it. However, don't you worry, my day for handling venomous snakes was on the horizon!

By the time I entered the ninth grade in Wichita Falls at the great Hirschi High School, beyond snakes, five things pretty much ruled my life: martial arts, band, basketball, dancing, and, like most normal teens, socializing. Although I had a short run at playing football in the eighth grade, my devotion to martial arts training ultimately won out, and my association with football forever came to an abrupt end. (To this day, unlike so many other Texans, I still do not "follow" football. It seems to me that many people actually worship this modern-day version of the gladiators, as well as some other sports, but hopefully you aren't one of them. I know I have gone to meddling, but I hope you'll forgive me.) As you can see from the list of my own particular pursuits, I had my own areas of behavioral concerns which needed to be addressed, and over time, these areas most assuredly have been. However, there is a reason I gave you my personal list, which will become apparent very soon…

Snakes You Can't See

At this point, it is important to note that while I did indeed continue to pursue my infatuation-turned-obsession with snakes, there were things happening to me back then that also had to do with snakes, but not ones that you can see with your physical eyes. There were snakes that were "sent" into my life from an early age, and the sender of those "invisible" snakes was not my loving Heavenly Father. These "snakes" were assigned to distract me from the things of God, to fill my mind with anything but the Word of God, and to keep me from connecting with the real plan of God for my life, which has been kept in store by God Himself since the foundation of the Earth.

As I journeyed through my high school years, snakes I could not see, recognize, understand, or effectively address, became increasingly active in my life. The direct consequences of their very real presence in my life began "manifesting" in all kinds of ways, all of which pointed to one specific evil architect. Satan, who has been clearly identified in the Bible, is *the* Snake (The Serpent in Genesis 3); and he sends his "snakes" into the lives of all Mankind for three reasons (which can easily be summarized into three simple but unambiguous words). The Word of God clearly tells us what those reasons are through the words of the Lord Jesus during His earthly ministry:

*"The thief does not come except to steal,
and to kill, and to destroy.
I have come that they may have life, and that
they may have it more abundantly."*
John 10:10

Just in case you missed it, the mission statement of hell is steal, kill, and destroy. In this life, for as long as we live, everything the enemy does in our lives revolves around these three words: steal, kill, and destroy. Unfortunately, where his mission is concerned, he is always "all in".

Overcoming the plans and tactics the enemy uses in our lives can never be accomplished without the illumination, direct intervention, and power of the Holy Spirit. He is completely aware of how the enemy operates (how he attacks, the devices that he uses, his plans, and his schemes). Not only that, since the Holy Spirit is part of the Godhead, the Trinity, He knows all the enemy is going to do *before* he does it. That is one of the reasons we so desperately need the Spirit of God in operation in our lives to the fullest extent possible. Oh, by the way, did you know that you can ask God for **more** of the Holy Spirit? That being said, what serious follower of the Lord Jesus Christ would not want more of Him, especially in these last days? (Please see Luke 11:13 for this revelation.) We all need more of Him. No one, and I mean not one person on the planet, operates in the Spirit to the fullest extent that is possible. True followers of Jesus understand the absolute necessity of having the Blood of the Lamb operating in our lives daily. You might check out some of the truths in the new Testament Book of 1 John Chapter One for more clarity and greater understanding in this area.

Simply put, the illuminating work of the Holy Spirit in our lives reveals truths to us that we would not have without Him. And while I personally do not encourage giving "spiritual" snakes that operate in our lives names (the Bible calls them "demons" or "devils"); sometimes it can be important to do so, to the end that we can understand more about how certain snakes operate in their warfare against us (Modus Operandi). Notwithstanding, I could easily identify more than one snake sent into my life by the Serpent when I was young. For the sake of brevity, let's look at the operation and manifestation of just one. Additionally, to keep confusion at bay, and to keep you and I on the same page, let's simply call this snake "Depression".

When Depression first surfaced in my life in my middle teens, do you think I knew what it was? If anyone had asked me at that time, "Darryl, do you know what depression is?" What do you think my answer would have been? If you had been me at fifteen or sixteen years old, having never heard about this malady before, nor known anyone who had it, what would your answer have been? Right now, can you truly recognize when Depression is tightening its' coils around you or one of your loved ones? Would you know what to do to defend yourself from this attack, or how to help someone else, if you did actually recognize this snake in operation for what it is?

The onset of most, if not all, depressive "episodes" that have occurred in my life were usually precipitated by an out-of-the-norm extreme event. At least that has been my very personal experience. (I am no expert by practice or profession, but I do have some understanding regarding my own personal life experiences, and the things that I have walked through.) If you are thinking that "extreme" is a relative term, you are so right. The same event can impact people differently. Much depends on who the person is, how they may "see" things, and how they may be "wired" internally. One additional factor, which remains largely unacknowledged in most ministries, is the number and types of "snakes" assigned to steal, kill, and destroy, especially in lives of believers who truly belong to the household of God; and who are actively and purposely seeking to advance His kingdom in these last days. It is not the same for everyone. This is spiritually mature subject matter, and not everyone is going to arrive at this understanding. Anyway, no matter "where" you are spiritually, or what you may believe, please, by all means, keep reading.

So, at fifteen, I experienced the abrupt and unexpected end of a very close personal friendship. The sudden loss of this relationship from my innermost circle of friends completely devastated me. I now understand that what happened to me afterward was deep depression. I had never felt so "low" before, and this loss was deeply disturbing to me. It took weeks for me to feel like my downward spiral was arrested, and for me to "find my footing", so that I could again try to enjoy life and feel "normal".

My obsession with snakes was not working for me. Band was both helpful (somewhat) and hurtful, because my friend whom I so deeply loved was in the same band class that I was. Basketball season was over, so no recovery was available for me on the "court". Martial Arts training was somewhat helpful, especially if I could engage in sparring. Do you think I understood that all the anger I felt for what I perceived as stolen from me in relationship was rooted in emotions based on chemicals reacting in my brain for which I had no positive outlet? Unfortunately for me, there was not a competent, **trustworthy** person that I could talk with about the depth of my pain. My dad was on TDY in Korea again, and he was unable to help me. My mom was available, but I certainly did not trust her. I turned sixteen before that school year ended, and that was how my sophomore year in high school came to a most undesirable end.

So, there I was at sixteen years old, wrestling with this snake called Depression, and I was just trying to survive the attack any way that I could. When I returned to Hirschi in the fall to start my junior year, I functioned somewhat better that school year, as much as I could, but there was still a lot of unshakeable sadness that I experienced because of the loss I endured just a few months before. I wish I could tell you that this one "episode" of depression was the only one I ever experienced. I wish I could tell you that this "snake" miraculously disappeared from my life leaving no trace. If I told you that, I would most assuredly be lying, because the next event soon to transpire involving the same type of "snake" (Depression) definitely proved to be much, much worse.

My junior year at Hirschi was bitterly interrupted by yet another military move. Up until this move, all preceding relocations had occurred during the summers between school years. This one was not to be, and it was the hardest one of all. My dad got new "Orders" to move to a place called Valdosta, Georgia, which is the home of Moody Air Force Base. I had never even heard of Valdosta before this time in my life. As I recall, I actually had to look it up on a map. Although I don't remember the exact dates of the move, we left Wichita Falls somewhere between the last two weeks of November and the first week of December 1979. The timing of this move absolutely could not have been more worse for me.

When Hirschi was notified that I was going to be removed from the school mid-year because of my dads' obligation to the military, things began to happen for which I did not have the position or the power to stop. Although I was able to finish the fall marching band season, I was prevented from even trying out for the varsity basketball team at Hirschi (which I had expected to do but for the move). To his credit, the coach talked to me about it, but it didn't stop me from feeling more sadness upon sadness. (Remember, I had not fully recovered from the life-altering event I had experienced just a few months before… I was still in significant pain.) I had to watch from the sidelines as friends I had played basketball with for the last three years took to the court in a game I had come to love. I do not have the words to tell you how hard that was to endure. However, what was happening in my life was much bigger than basketball. After all the military relocations I had endured, I had finally found a "home", a place where I truly felt like I was accepted, belonged, and loved, and now we were once again moving.

I still remember, like it was yesterday, the fateful night we drove away from Wichita Falls. Even after all these years (today is Friday, December the 28th, 2018, and I am now 55 years old), as I am writing this paragraph, the fountain has broken, and the tears are streaming down my face. I do not know why it still hurts to this day. I guess I still feel in my heart how much I may have missed in relationships, and most of what I had back then was never replaced (we only go through our high school "season" once). How fragile this life is, and how important it is to cherish who we do have in our lives, as those relationships can never be replaced. I am talking about close, loving, healthy relationships. I still have my Letter Jacket from the Northwest Junior High. I still have my 1979 Husky Band shirt. I still have the first Bible I remember being given to me from a faithful and wonderful friend named "Kit". It's the people that I have lost, the relationships, and some of them have now left this life forever. I will never ever see them again unless…

What I am trying to show you is that my heart was fully-engaged with where I was in life. And if you haven't figured this out yet, when your heart is engaged, and you are "all in", then you are vulnerable to being injured. It is hard to be injured if your heart is that of stone, and you're not engaged in the relationships that God has blessed you with. A failure to engage can also be due to how deep you are "lost in the forest" of life. Not only can you be hurt by people (none of us are perfect, and it is just part of livin' in a fallen world), but you are also vulnerable to the enemy of our souls. Satan is a real spiritual entity, and he can hurt you by manifesting hell in your life in ways too numerous to count. This thing called life is not a game. If you can imagine someone who, with all of their being is "all in" about killing and destroying you, multiply that by a hundred or even a thousand, and you've got Satan. If you think of life as a game, Steal, Kill, and Destroy is the name of his game. He has been at it for a long time, and unfortunately for Mankind, he is astoundingly good at it. Do you really want to squander your life away playing his game? (Please say, "NO!")

The good news is that we are not without hope. No matter what adversity, no matter what difficulty we may face in this life, no matter what we may have done in the past, Jesus Christ is the answer! Did you catch the second part of the verse we looked at earlier in the Book of John?

"...I have come that they may have life, and that they may have it more abundantly."
John 10:10b

Wow! What a declaration of the Lord Jesus! In the first half of the verse, we saw the mission of hell (steal, kill, and destroy). But in the second half we see one of the great mission statements of God through Jesus.

At this point, I would be remiss if I failed to provide a short list of areas in our lives where snakes commonly operate to carry out the mission of hell in all Mankind, which, as has already been stated, is to steal, kill, and destroy. This list is not a guarantee that spiritual snakes are in actual operation all the time when what represents these areas is identified. If the stronghold has effectively been set up in a person's life, it does the job for hell whether or not demons are actively engaged in their evil operations. Also, this list is not exhaustive by any means. An exhaustive list would take up an entire resource by itself. This is **a** list, not **the** list. And the order is alphabetical, and not in order of importance. Let us begin…

Anger
Anxiety
Argumentative
Astrology
Boasting
Blasphemers
Brutality
Complacency
Conceit
Contentions
Corruption
Covetousness
Deception
Depression
Despisers of Good
Dissentions
Drugs (Illegal and Illicit)
Drunkenness
Elitism
Entertainment

Envy
Evil Thoughts
False Witness
Fantasizing
Foolishness
Gambling
Greed
Hatred
Haughtiness
Headstrong
Heresies
Horoscopes
Human Trafficking
Idolatry
Imaginations (Evil)
Immorality
Iniquities
Itching Ears
Jealousy
Judgmental Attitudes
Lewdness
*Licentiousness   (Definition on Page 39.)
Lying
Love of Bloodshed
Love of Money
Masonry (Occult)
Materialism
Mockeries
Murder
Nicotine
Nosiness
Nonchalance
Occult
Order of the Eastern Star

Outbursts of Wrath
Paranoia
Perversity
Pleasure
Pornography
Pride
Profanity
Proud
Quarrelsome
Racism
Rage
Revelries
Secret Societies
Selfish Ambition
Self-Love
Sensuality
Sexual Sins
Slander
Slavery
Spiritual Immaturity
Sorcery
Sports
Tattoos
Theft
Unbelief
Uncleanness
Uncorrectable
Unforgiving
Unholy
Unreceptive to Rebukes/Reproofs
Unthankful
Wickedness
Witchcraft
Worldliness

There you have it. Again, this list is not at all exhaustive, but every single one of us, including me, can find something on that list in which we have behaved at one point or another. Most of us, including me, could probably identify more than one something. But Georgia is on my mind, so let's get back to my unhappy and unwanted arrival to the Peach State.

Valdosta, Georgia

Even though I gave considerable thought to entering the Military when I graduated from high school, the living situation we encountered when we arrived in Valdosta definitely gave me considerable pause. I really hope that no other families encountered what we encountered upon our arrival. You would think that whoever oversaw logistics for service members would be on top of their game when it came to relocating entire families from one base to another. When we arrived in Valdosta, the base did not have housing ready and available for our family. So, my parents, along with their three teenage children, all lived in a one-room, one-bathroom hotel on Ashley Boulevard for not one, not two, but three entire months! That was, in itself, absolutely demoralizing. Could this situation have contributed to depression? I am sure that it did. However, I assign no blame to either of my parents for the move itself, or for how things were when we arrived. It was not their fault. But fault or no fault, the constricting coils of Depression became the worse I had ever experienced.

Over the next three months, the Serpent did his utmost to squeeze the life right out of me. I was very hard-pressed to move forward with any area of my life in that season. Again, none of the things that used to bring me joy did. For the first time in my life, I did not want to live. The pit of depression into which I had been dragged was so deep, I was in grave danger. The thoughts that the enemy planted in my head of wanting to prematurely depart this planet had everything to do with the amount of pain I was enduring because of the move, as well as other previous gut-wrenching experiences. The primary reason I did not take any active steps to bring about my own demise was simply my own ignorance about how to do it, and the capability to do it. Thank God for my ignorance and inability!

Perhaps here is a good place to share with you a little more about the tactics of the enemy in life. Whether acting alone, or in concert with other "snakes" (demons), the desired end of the snake of Depression is death. That is the primary operational strategy of this snake. There is a snake called Suicide, and guess what its' job is? It always operates to put thoughts in your head about ending your life. Nowadays, when you watch the news, too often to recount you see the snake of Suicide working in concert with a snake called Murder. These wicked spirits work through people to get them to murder innocent victims, and then they lead them to take their own life to avoid capture or consequences. This is certainly **not** the case with most suicides, but it is far too common. Since this is not a treatise on suicide or related deaths, I will continue moving forward.

However, I do want to say a little more about depression. Did you know that when a person is depressed for an extended period of time (experts vary on this, but 2-3 weeks is a commonly accepted time frame), chemical balances in the brain are unhealthily disrupted, and the person suffering it is *usually* not ever the same afterwards? This can, and I emphasize can, have long-term impact in the life of the one suffering the depression. I was not aware of this truth until over twenty-five years after my first "bout" with this device of the enemy. In point of fact, I suffered two long-lasting depression events in the same year (1979). The first one lasted well over two weeks, but the second one lasted around three months, before I was final able to rise above a desire to prematurely eject from this life.

Now, the sentence you just read does not have the correct understanding regarding how my situation was resolved. In fact, it had much less to do with what "I" did, and way more to do with what God did in the beginning of my life. The Lord graciously gifted me with musical talent, and the band at Lowndes High School was where God gave me a measure of restoration through new friends that I met at my new high school. There I received strength to keep moving forward in life. It was not a great amount of strength, mind you, but it was enough to keep going. Sometimes all we get is "just enough", but that just enough is enough.

Regarding my continued pursuit of my obsession with real-world snakes, perhaps you are wondering if I had any new experiences with actual physical specimens while in Valdosta? Well, I did indeed. One afternoon I was out snake hunting, and I caught two (2) snakes on the same hunt. That had never happened to me before. Good thing I had two pillowcases to contain them separately. They needed to be separate because one (an Eastern King Snake) most likely would have tried to eat the other one (a Black Racer). That day still stands out somewhat in my memory, but the "snakes" that are sent to steal, kill, and destroy in your life and in mine are really what this resource is about. While identifying the snakes presents the problem, we all face, I believe with all my heart that there is only one Solution. And make no mistake about it, **He is** the Message of this book.

"For I am not ashamed of the gospel of Christ,
for it is the power of God to salvation
for everyone who believes,
for the Jew first and also for the Greek.
For in it the righteousness of God
is revealed from faith to faith;
as it is written,
'The just shall live by faith.'"
Romans 1:16, 17

Chapter Five

The Madness Continued in College!

Towards the end of my senior year in high school (in Valdosta), I began considering, as most teenagers do, what I might do after graduation. The only two viable options before me, I believed, were to go to college or go into the Armed Forces. The college option was a continuation in my pursuit of Herpetology, but the Military was not. So, I was considering two completely different career paths. However, a "power play" by my mother (not my father) caused me to choose college; because, in truth, I really was leaning more towards the Military, like my father before me. Anyway, tuition costs led me to choose a college in the state of Alabama, in the city of Troy, called Troy State University. (It's now just Troy University.) I applied and was accepted. So, in the fall off to college I went. And true to the answer I had given for several years about my occupational direction, Biology was recorded as my major, pursuant to becoming a Herpetologist. The Science building became my new home, but at that time my pursuit of snakes still had competition for my time due to my continued interest in band. But all that was just about to change.

Since I still had a desire to participate in marching band, I had to be at school earlier than other students for "band camp". However, I soon felt like a fish out of water, because the largest percentage of musicians which participated in the band were music majors, and I definitely was not. I had no intention to even minor in music, let alone major in it; so, this unique environment complicated things for me. The reason this became an issue for me is because music majors loved to practice. And this was especially true of the percussion section (of which I was a part as I played "quads"). I enjoyed practicing too, to an extent, but I had a life outside of music, and soon section rehearsals got all over my nerves. Additionally, at TSU football games, whenever our team would score a touchdown, the band had to play the "fight" song which was "Dixie". Needless to say, I hated that song every time we played it, and I still do. (If you have to ask why…) Thus, this came to be the end of band for me. The last significant marching band memory for me was marching in the annual Blue/Grey Football Game in Montgomery Alabama (1981). So, I finally retired my drumsticks while at Troy State University. There was some sadness regarding my decision, since I had been a percussionist since the fifth grade, but I have absolutely no regrets about closing that door in my life at that time.

Now that my long-time interest in snakes had its' primary competition moved out of the way, I plunged much deeper into my obsession. My no-fear attitude (the Bible calls that pride, and it truly does go before the fall) had now taken me to a place where I was ready to indulge in even more risky behavior involving snakes. Before this time in my life, I had never ever attempted to handle in any way a venomous snake. I considered all of that as part of my juvenile existence package, and I was now "grown". I truly felt like I was ready to take this next deadly step; I just needed the opportunity to apply my great herpetological understanding. I've heard that there is a popular "proverb" which says, "Be careful of what you wish for…" Well, my long-held deeply desired "wish" for my first opportunity to handle a venomous snake finally presented itself at my college of choice in the Science building.

Before classes even began, I made my way to the Science building to see what animals were on hand to "study". As I walked through the main entrance of the building that first day, to my left I observed a large glass front enclosure, and guess what was in it? Yes, it was a snake, and it wasn't just any snake either! It was a large (five to five and a half feet long as I recall) Eastern Diamondback Rattlesnake (*Crotalus adamanteous*). To say I was most excited, again, is an understatement. To think that I might have access to working with this "beautiful" creature was almost beyond belief.

As my mind raced, I realized that I had to find whoever was in charge of that display, make my wishes known to the powers that were, and see if I could be granted access to pursue my desire. I quickly located the university staff member with the power to grant me access, and I unapologetically made my wishes known. I was granted access on the spot, and was given the keys to the kingdom, or "cagedom", as it were. (Yes, I made that one up!). Please understand that I am not mocking God or the Holy Bible by saying that. I'm trying to show you how far in the pit I had gone in the derangement of my juvenile thinking.

Anyhow, now that I finally had an opportunity to work with venomous snakes, I couldn't wait to get started. Although I was new to this lethal activity, I certainly wanted to be as professional as I could, so my first task was to find a snake "stick" so that I could safely handle my new work "partner". Without any previous training from a professional, and without anyone watching my back, so to speak, at eighteen I made the jump, and had my first physical interaction with a rattlesnake. The experience was absolutely exhilarating! (I didn't know that the "high" I was feeling was from the adrenaline released into my system due to the inherent danger of being in close proximity to an animal obviously built for the kill. Besides being obsessed with snakes, I was also on the road to becoming an adrenaline "junkie".) Once again, I was "all in", and became even more entrenched in my obsession. (That's another way of saying that I became more of a "captive" to it. And Jesus came to set the captives free!) I had other close encounters with that same rattlesnake, but the twists and turns of chasing my obsession were about to go even deeper.

Along with all the other things on the table of my life my first year in college, there was also an inner longing to continue receiving some level of spiritual impartation for life guidance and direction. I had begun some level of regularly attending a bible study while in Wichita Falls. I had continued this exercise in Valdosta, with an organization on the base called Protestant Youth of the Church. So, at TSU a church near the campus to attend was located, and I began regularly attending it. I began routinely receiving instruction from the Word of God, and my spiritual understanding began to slowly grow. Then in the spring of 1982, I finally came to know Jesus Christ as my personal Savior. I repented of my sins, believed Who He is; accepted what He had done for me at Calvary; confessed my belief and allegiance to Him before a whole congregation; was buried with Him in the waters of baptism (my second time), and I was born again! Deep on the inside I slowly began to change. I want to emphasize the word "slowly". Walking by faith was never meant to be a solo endeavor. I wish a mature godly man had cared enough about me to **disciple** me. I wish my first year in Christ had been steeped in the painful spiritual process of **dying to myself**. Over the next few years at Troy State, not only did my friends come to know about my undying obsession with snakes, but so did my church family. Two particular situations stand out as stark memories of the descent of my unnatural devotion to snakes.

The first situation developed because a sweet couple at the church I attended knew that I was "into" snakes. One day, this precious sister reported to me that her husband had been out riding a horse on some property the day before, and that he had seen a large rattlesnake crawl into a partially submerged aluminum drainage pipe. She asked me if I was interested in catching it to add to the collection of the college. Not only did she not have to ask me twice, but after my joyful response to her question, I quickly asked her a question. I blurted out, "When are we going?" This adventure was scheduled for the very next day. I certainly did not want to miss this fantastic opportunity!

The following afternoon, I was picked up and driven out to the property where this snake had been sighted. I had been led to believe that it was of a significant size, so I truly was excited. I had with me all the equipment you would expect a professional herpetologist to have with one exception. I still did not have appropriate first aid equipment of any kind on my person, nor did I have anti-venom. Does it sound to you like I was prepared for any eventuality?

Well, when I arrived at the spot where the drainage pipe was, the first thing that I noticed was that one end of the pipe was completely underground, and the other end was canted at an upward angle with the opening sitting about halfway above the ground. At this point, I wasn't sure how far down into the ground the pipe went, nor was I sure how much daylight made it into the pipe. I bent down to look into the pipe, and just about two or three feet in, I could clearly see the outline of a rather sizeable snake sitting in the pipe. The question in my mind now became, "How was I going to get that snake, whatever kind it was, out of that pipe?"

The very thought of catching this snake, no matter what kind it turned out to be, had my mind racing. Did you know that when you are in that type of excited state, sometimes you don't make your best decisions? Well, I just had to capture that snake. So, I figured out that since the snake was only a couple of feet inside the pipe, three at the most, if I pulled up on the exposed end of the pipe hard enough, it should probably give me enough clearance to capture the prize. Of course, the dilemma I then found myself in had to do with the "how". How do I pull up on the pipe using just my hand(s), without getting bitten? At this point, getting bit was a really small insignificant detail. Do you think I cared? Not really! I was not going to be denied my prize no matter what it cost me. Remember the list in chapter four where we saw pride identified as a snake? Well, there it is!

I wasted no time putting my plan into action. I placed my hand (I don't remember if it was one or both) on the end of that pipe and pulled it upwards with all my might. That pipe came up with such force, it completely cleared the spot where the snake was sitting, and for the first time, I saw what kind of snake it was. To my idiotic surprise, I had unearthed a rattlesnake! It was what was called at that time (and it may still be currently) a Canebrake Rattlesnake; and it was over three feet long. It had a diameter of at least three inches, so this was quite a healthy adult specimen. When I was a herpetologist back then this species was classified as a sub-species of the Timber Rattlesnake (*Crotalus horridus horridus*), but I won't go into the differences here. I want to finish sharing my story with you, because now things became really interesting.

You don't have to be rocket scientist to figure out that this snake had no interest in being captured. In fact, it had the audacity to attempt to escape me. Man, I wasn't even havin' that! As the snake quickly began crawling deeper in the pipe towards the still submerged end, I had a problem that had to be solved very quickly or I was going to lose my prize. Even though I had a snake stick to "pin" down his head for the grab, its' head was no longer in view. It was quickly disappearing down the pipe, and my opportunity to catch my first rattlesnake was also disappearing down that pipe with it. So, what do think I did?

I did what any serious herpetologist about to make history with his first capture of a venomous snake would do. I grabbed that monster by the tail! I then pulled it back out of that pipe, where the "fight" to get it into my bag was now "on". After a few harrowing seconds of trying to maneuver this rattler into a position where I was finally able to pin its head down, I got it! With my prize safely in the bag, I was driven back to the campus where it was joyfully added to the collection. That was the first rattlesnake I caught in the wild. On a side note, handling this particular snake gave me a surprising personal introduction to a new-to-me previously unexperienced defensive adaptation called "musk glands", which to me smelled like dirty socks. (Don't bother sniffing yours; it's not the same!) Sometime later this rattlesnake was safely released back into the wild in a different area. However, this snake, and the other rattler I mentioned earlier in this chapter helped me to create an even more dangerous, albeit sometimes humorous (to me anyway), situation where I ate, slept, and lived.

It's one thing to work with venomous snakes and enjoy it. Lunacy on a whole deeper level exists when you choose to have venomous snakes where you live. That in itself is dangerous to the "nth" degree. Anyone who feels that this level of obsessive behavior is acceptable, and within what may be called "normal", has some issues with their internal hard drive (the brain). It's not like having a piranha in an aquarium at your house. If the piranha escapes, there probably won't be any injuries to your neighbors. The piranha can't crawl under the fence, stealthily enter your neighbors' house, and bite someone. But a venomous snake certainly can. Anyone who tells you that there is either a low level of danger or none at all is an absolute idiot. Please don't even bother about trying to persuade me otherwise; it would be a ridiculous waste of your time and mine.

So, I definitely did not have a firm grasp on reality when I decided that I could "care" for these two rattlesnakes better in my dorm room (off-campus) than in the science building. And I had a roommate who was definitely not into snakes at all. Do you think I had any concern for his welfare at that time in my life? Do you think I had any knowledge of legal responsibilities and civil liability at that time in my life? You may be wondering just how could I find anything even remotely humorous about this situation? Well, it was one of those middle-of-the-night kinds of things…

Imagine you're asleep. You wake up in the middle of the night, say two or three o'clock, to visit the restroom. You struggle out of your bed, get your feet situated on the floor, stand up, and start walking. About your third or fourth step, you are horrified to hear an unmistakable sound. It's the calling card of a killing machine in alarm mode. You hear what you know is the rattle of a rattlesnake. You stop in your tracks to ascertain how close this unwelcome creature is to you. You quickly remember that your demented roommate

80

has two "pet" rattlesnakes in a cage just a few feet away, and the alarm that was just initiated when you started walking and became suddenly startled, has your roommate laughing. I don't care what anybody else says about it. That clown (talking about me and meaning no disrespect to any real clowns) had an obsession, and it was no little thing. Again, endangering yourself or others to have what you want is not in any way normal behavior. It is an obsession, and the person captive to it seriously needs help. And this applies to any type of obsessive behavior, although some, I will admit, are inherently more dangerous than others.

The stories I have shared with you are not all the stories I have in my memory about my experiences with snakes when I was in college. I didn't even touch on my first experience of "milking" one of the rattlesnakes without any protective oversight, and how that one almost "nailed" me while doing it. The whole point of my sharing what I did is to prompt you into thinking about your own behaviors, and whether or not you may have an obsession that may need to be addressed in your own life, for your sake as well as others. It's now time to switch gears, so to speak, in order to take the next step in the evolution of my obsession with snakes. But before I do, please allow me to set the stage.

There is an interesting phenomenon that happens to race-horses when the time for them to run draws close. When the horse is lead into the chute at the starting line, sometimes a horse looks like it goes "crazy" in the chute. With the rider mounted, the horse starts jumping up and down, sometimes even bucking in the chute, right before the race starts. I never pursued that obsessive activity, but I have seen this phenomenon on television. I mention it because more than once in my life, I have been like that horse. I just couldn't wait to get out of my "chute" to start running. That's exactly where I was my senior year in college. I was tired of school, tired of sitting in classes, and tired of not "living my dream". I was ready for a change, and the change brought me back west to the state of Texas.

Of course, for the life-altering change I was seeking to occur, I had to first locate a place that had an entry-level opening for which I could apply. As I began to actively seek such a place in the Fall of 1984, I made a few a few phone calls to zoos in Texas (where I had enjoyed living the most), and I found out that the Dallas Zoo had open at that time the exact position for which I was looking. Why does it seem that with every wonderful opportunity, circumstances that may not be the most preferable come with it? The position was open in the fall, but I wasn't scheduled to graduate from TSU until the following spring. What's an upwardly mobile young man to do?

After giving the situation significant consideration, I decided to go ahead and pursue the position with the Dallas Zoo. I reasoned that if I ended up not being selected for that position, then I would stay on track towards finishing my degree, while seeking another position elsewhere. Well, I submitted my application (actual paper back then), and I was contacted by the Reptile Department for an in-person interview. The interview was scheduled, and I made the appointment. I was given an insider tour of the Snake House (which was way too "cool"!), and afterwards I made the trip back to college.

Within a few weeks, I was finally notified that I had indeed been hired for the position! I made the necessary preparations for my Dallas Zoo appear-by date, while I finished my last quarter at college (Troy State was not a semester program school back then). At the end of the quarter, I returned to Valdosta where I celebrated Thanksgiving with my family. The next day, my brother and one of his friends, drove me out to Dallas, and dropped me off (with very little of my belongings) at a hotel on the south side of the city. Such was the beginning of my "career" as a Herpetologist, and just like the racehorse that I referred to earlier, man was I excited! My dream had come true! Praise the Lord? Maybe not…

The above photo was taken by the author. It is the lost rattle (through shedding not death) of a captive mature Eastern Diamondback Rattlesnake. It was approximately six and a half feet long and was quite the specimen to behold!

(The business card is included in the photo
purely as a reference for scale.)

Part Three: Freedom!

"Then Jesus said to those Jews who believed Him, 'If you abide in My Word, you are My disciples indeed.
*"And you shall know the **truth**, and the **truth** shall make you **free**.*
*"Therefore **if** the son makes you **free**, you shall be **free** indeed."*
John 8:31-32, 36
(Emphasis added.)

This graphic is a compilation of two photographs of the identification and employer position patches from a zoo uniform shirt worn by the author in 1985. The shirt itself will be "showcased" video graphically, both on my Amazon Author Page and my website: darrylhornwrites.com...

Lord Willing!

Chapter Six

Snakes As a Career?

After arriving in the big City of Dallas, the very first thing I did Sunday morning, was walk in search of a church to attend. I happened upon Marsalis Avenue, after walking from Loop 12. The first church I came to was Marsalis Avenue Church of Christ. I enjoyed that first service tremendously (for where I was spiritually then), and I made this strong congregation my church home. It remained so until I moved from Dallas to Fort Worth four years later. After connecting with MACC, my next task was to set up house. I settled into an apartment in Oak Cliff. I can still remember the address to this day. It was an upstairs apartment on Eighth Avenue (422). That building is no longer there, but my memories of it are still vivid. From its' balcony, I enjoyed a beautiful unobstructed view of downtown Dallas. Since I was an avid runner back then, I developed a habit of getting up early in the morning to run. I would run down Marsalis Avenue, across the bridge into downtown Dallas, and then back across the bridge to my apartment before going to work. I enjoyed being in my "zone". This pre-dawn activity was very unsafe, and I certainly would not recommend it today.

So, my first real job as a Reptile Keeper, a professional herpetologist, started November of 1984. This was the life that I had dreamed of ever since I was kid! This was the first time (and last) that I worked with such a large and varied herpetological collection. Most of what was in the building I had never "handled" before. Remember me mentioning something about not having a firm grasp on reality? The revelation that I didn't have a firm grasp began to become clearly evident not long after I started working there. I have to say at the outset, that there was never a day that I disliked or had problems with any of the people I had the honor of working with. My downfall is that I unwittingly chose the wrong occupation. All my coworkers were both helpful and supportive; I appreciated every one of them and enjoyed the comradery we shared working together. So, what was it like working with snakes at the zoo?

A typical day at the zoo, as a Reptile Keeper, began like most other jobs. There was a time to arrive (eight hours on the clock), and a time to depart. I liked the mornings the best. This is because upon arrival, after a cursory walk-through of the snake house and its' inhabitants, particularly the animals assigned for your particular care, all those present that day would go to a central location behind-the-scenes, and out-of-the-publics' eye or access, for coffee at a table, and a little more time to wake up. How can someone still be sleepy working around animals that could hurt you bad, or even kill you? Here we are back to that reality check again!

Anyway, at the table would be all kinds of discussion that centered around not just animals in the building but herpetology in general. The overall health of the collection was always in the discussion. Challenges presented by captive animals were also shared in the hope that solutions for their care could be realized. And any issues that could even remotely be considered dangerous to us, the keepers, were always addressed. Of course, there was more reading undertaken to continue adding to my herpetological knowledge. After I had been there for a couple of weeks, there was also a special type of "pop quiz" regarding one of my coworkers having been bitten by one of our venomous charges, and more specifically my response to it. This test of my understanding was training for the unthinkable, and was critically important for the following reasons…

In case you have ever wondered if the snakes we had in the collection still had their fangs, most assuredly, they did. Fangs were not pulled or surgically removed in any way. Any of those types of "render-them-harmless" approaches were and are considered barbaric by professionals. All the snakes in our collection had their killing equipment intact. And, yes, we did have snakes in the building which, if you were bitten, could kill you in minutes without anti-venom (antivenin). Of course, I'm thinking particularly of the quick-to-be-agitated Black Mamba of Africa. We actually had two Mamba's, but they were never "handled". They were too quick and agile, and their neurotoxic venom would have you in convulsions on the floor in minutes; and dead within the hour, if you were bitten by either of them. Other most notable extremely dangerous specimens were Central American Bushmasters, Australian Death Adders, and the venerable Gaboon Vipers also of Africa.

However, the venomous snakes weren't the only ones that were dangerous. One of my "charges" as the low keeper on the totem pole (newest employee) was a giant twenty-six-foot Reticulated Python (*Python Reticulatus*). I had never worked with a snake that large before, and boy, was it massive! I had affectionately given this snake the nickname of "Popeye", because to me it looked like the snakes' eyes bugged out. During my time at the zoo, we only took that snake out of its' cage once. It took four of is to handle it, and that was no easy matter. It has been documented that a snake that size can easily kill an adult man with little difficulty by constriction. Here's a simple explanation of how the constriction killing method works.

When a snake that has constriction-capability takes hold of its' prey (food), immediately following the strike, that is the bite, it quickly wraps two or three coils around the animal it has caught. The snake then quickly tightens its' muscles to negatively affect the breathing of the animal to the creatures' demise. When the animal exhales, the snake tightens its' coils even more, so the animal can't inhale. The poor creature slowly suffocates to death. After that comes the infamous swallow-it-whole activity, which can take some time depending on the size of the animals involved. Needless to say, this would not be an "enjoyable" way to depart from planet Earth.

So then, why was I in a cage with this dinosaur-size snake one day at the zoo? The easy answer is because it was my job. The difficulty lies in the fact that there was one occasion when it did indeed bite me (I still have visible scars from the encounter on my right hand to this day), and the whole scenario was unforgettable. I learned a lot about people that day, and I have never forgotten what I learned. That's the day I became keenly aware of how sadistic people can be. Who wants a normal, boring day at the zoo? Not much in the way of conversation there. "Yeah, I went to the zoo Saturday, saw some snakes, and it sure was cool." How boring is that? Compare it to this: "Yeah, I went to the zoo Saturday, and when I was in the snake house you would not believe what happened! Man, I saw this dude working in this cage with an unbelievably huge python and it bit him!" You can get a tremendous amount of conversational fodder out of that second statement; much more so than the first. But let me tell you the whole story…

It was a normal day in the snake house. There wasn't anything ominous about it that would have let me know that this particular day would be vastly different. As usual, there were quite a few folks checking out the snakes and other "critters" in our collection. I was used to small crowds gathering in front of the python cage whenever I physically went in there. This day I needed to clean (squeegee) the glass for captive enclosure cleanliness as well as to provide better observational opportunities for the viewing public. This snake had never been a problem before (that I knew of), and there was nothing presented to me that day to make me think that there would even be a problem. I was completely unprepared for what was about to happen.

The snake was coiled up and laying on the floor of the cage up against the glass. As I wiped the glass above where it lay, everything seemed to begin moving in slow motion. (This was my first experience of a phenomenon called "Tachypsychia"; an unusual condition where one sees or experiences events in slow motion in their mind even though in reality things are happening very, very fast.) I saw the massive head of this snake rising towards my hand with its' cavernous mouth wide open. I knew the bite was coming, so I tried to move my hand out of the way by retracting it (it was extended to the glass), but I wasn't quite fast enough. I felt the mouth of this beast "graze" my hand but thank God it did not get a hold of me. It slowly retracted its' head to a coiled position, and then watched me with a sinister stare. That is the one time in my life I felt like an over-sized rodent that barely escaped imminent death by a natural world "monster". I don't think it could have eaten me, but I certainly did not want to find out if it could.

As I came to an awareness of what had just happened, I felt blood running down my arm. I took a close look at my right hand and saw several (6-8) distinct "slash" marks where the teeth of this snake had entered my hand. While assessing what had happened, and anxiously considering what might happen next, I became keenly aware of much commotion in front of the cage. I could then hear the excitement-rich statements of those who had just seen what had happened calling others to the scene of the crime. I'm quite certain there was an immense desire on the part of some of the viewers to see more "action". See what I mean by sadistic? I didn't see anybody out there praying for me. And this was something I really needed because I was still in "striking" range. Some naysayers might say, "Well if you're stupid enough to be in there..." There is a high probability that they might be right about that.

I then made a quality decision to exit the cage while I still could, address my wounds, and then figure out what to do about that Behemoth of a reptile. I'm sure there's at least one reader who is thinking, "It's time to make some boots out of that snake." Well, that may have happened one day (long after I resigned), but it didn't happen that day. I had to finish my job. As I cleaned my hand and applied first aid bandages, I gave a lot of thought to what happened, and how I could prevent a repeat performance (despite the fact that the onlookers outside the cage probably would have loved to see the snake bite me again). It occurred to me that maybe I startled the python by my movement directly over it.

After a few minutes of careful consideration, I decided to put a trash can lid over the snake, which was still in a coiled position by the glass right where I left all my cleaning supplies. So that's what I did. I crawled back into that cage, and placed a trash can lid over the python, and continued with my work. Now remember, we're talking about being in close quarters with a long-time captive animal that still maintained its' natural killing instincts. It's not like the python "loved" me and wanted to be good buddies with me. It's not like I worked at a department store, and a box fell off the shelf and bit me. This snake could have easily killed me, and to do so was just a decision on its' part. Also, emergency notification measures in lethal environments back then were not what they might be today. In other words, there wasn't a button I could immediately push to let my co-workers know that I was in trouble and needed immediate assistance; otherwise, yours truly was going to transform into a big lump inside the stomach of a super-predator. Now, it may seem to you that I'm simply telling you a story to entertain you. I look back now, and I know God was with me, and that is the only reason I'm alive today. It wasn't about my great snake-handling skills. I was caught in a spiritual battle in the heavenlies between the God of heaven and earth and the Serpent.

If you were to ask me if I were bitten by any other snakes while I worked there, I would answer in the affirmative. A large Cuban Boa left its' calling card on the outside of my left index finger, and those scars are still visible too. But thank God, I was never bitten by any type of venomous snake while employed at the zoo, although there were several close calls. The most alarming close call happened the last week I worked there. It involved a "feeding response" from a large Water Moccasin, and it came just inches from nailing my face. Had I indeed been bitten, it definitely would be categorized as operator, or keeper as it were, error. The snake would not have been the blame. It was only doing what snakes do.

So let me now interject a couple of questions for you to consider. What is in your life right now that you are totally comfortable with that can really hurt you or someone you care about? I had become very comfortable (complacent) in the cage with that python, but that doesn't mean that it did not have the natural capacity to destroy me. You can say what you want, but I do not believe we have multiple opportunities at this thing called life. Obsessive behavior is not ever going to have your best interests at heart. Whatever your obsession is, it will always steal, kill, and destroy in your life and the lives of those around you. Being without understanding about this can/will automatically set yourself up to be destroyed. However, it doesn't have to be this way. You do have the power of choice.

Perhaps you may be wondering if I encountered any spiritual snakes while I worked with the physical ones at the zoo? The answer is "Yes". Remember in Chapter Four I went to great length to describe, identify, and name the snake called "Depression"? Well, this "attachment" re-surfaced in my life at the zoo. It launched its' attack the day I had an epiphany about the direction of my life. Sometimes when we engage in an activity that is so routine (for us anyway), we can carry out the monotonous task physically while thinking about other things. Well, one day I was doing my routine tasks, but I was thinking about my future, and I had several questions at the forefront of my thinking. "Is this it?" "Is this what my life is really about?" "Is this what I'm going to be doing for the next twenty or thirty years of my life?" "Do I want to spend the next thirty years of my life playing with snakes?" "Is this all life has for me?" My meditation on these and other questions led me to a deep and regretful awareness that somewhere along the way, I had missed "it". I had missed my true calling and had believed the lie that my life was only about snakes. In the midst of this "storm" of thoughts and feelings I was experiencing, guess who showed up? The snake of Depression again raised its' ugly head in my life and dragged me down into the pit again. But whereas the depression I had experienced at seventeen lasted about three months, this time I keenly remember it lasting four to six months.

For the first time in my life, I knew that my infatuation with snakes, my obsession, was not what my life was about. I did not want to spend the next thirty years of my life working with snakes. But in my eyes, I had a huge problem. What was I going to do now? Everything I had done since I was a child was geared towards me becoming a herpetologist and working with snakes. IBM didn't need my masterful snake-handling skills. Xerox wasn't looking for anyone who could extract venom from Cobras. I lost all my footing, all my direction in life, and depression again took me captive for a season. I must note that although I was deeply depressed, this time I had no desire to leave planet Earth. There were others in my life at that time and their care was supremely important. Finally, it was no longer all about me.

For months it became very difficult to function. I found myself sleeping ten to twelve hours a day. On days that I had to work, I barely got up in time to get to work. When my workday ended, I would go home, eat something, and would very soon be back in bed to sleep another twelve hours. Other things in which I had found much joy now only offered minimal positivity as the coils of Depression tightened around me more and more. By the time my one-year anniversary of working at the zoo came, I knew that I did not want to be a herpetologist for the rest of my life. It was time to find a new occupation. As that door began to close (inside me), new doors began to open.

To make a long story short, I finally quit the zoo to sell encyclopedias (New Standard). I enjoyed this new job immensely, as I truly felt like I was helping families by providing access to knowledge for their children. Today, with the proliferation of the Internet and all things technological, reading an actual book seems like the stone age to some. But reading encyclopedias was something I absolutely loved to do when I was a kid. However, there was not enough financial stability in what I was now doing in order to move forward in life. More career changes continued to occur, but this was the end of my career in Herpetology. Finally, snakes were no longer the focus of my life. I took my knowledge and experience with me, but not the love. My decision gave me some measure of freedom from a completely misdirected life in the pursuit of that which clearly represents the Serpent.

Chapter Seven

The Last Bite – Then Freedom

Several years ago, in a small Texas town called Meridian, I was driving on a familiar residential road. Since I was driving so slowly (it was daylight, and there was no other vehicular traffic to contend with), I spotted a suspicious looking "stick" on the road in front of me. It was suspicious looking because I thought it might be a snake. I slowed down a little bit more to confirm or deny my suspicions. When I was pretty certain it was a snake, I stopped, put my vehicle in park, exited and approached what I truly hoped would be a snake. Turns out I was right! It was a snake! It was a non-venomous Texas Rat Snake (*Elaphe obsoleta lindheimeri*) about two feet long.

Well, I didn't want the "little guy" to get run over or devoured by ravenous neighborhood domestic cats (of which there were plenty). So, I took it into protective custody and returned to my vehicle. I quickly obtained a container to put it in, so I could transport it to a safer, more remote location for release, in the hope that this harmless creature might be able to live a long, prosperous life killing rodents. Although this variety is quite useful to have around (because they are living nightmares to rodents), its' chances for survival would be much better somewhere else. To that end, I hand-carried it to the house, and secured a container in which to transport my temporary captive. The snake had seemed to be quite docile during this whole time. But you never know what a snake might be thinking, right?

To my unbelievable surprise, when I went to place it in the container, that joker bit me! What was so surprising to me was that this one bite drew blood (mine not "his"), and not just a little bit either. My new wound had to be washed with antiseptic and covered with a band-aid to stop the bleeding. I couldn't believe it. I had been bitten by far larger snakes than it at the Dallas Zoo (back in the day) that hadn't caused nearly as much fuss. To make another long story short, I did get this feisty creature with an attitude into the container (no thanks to it), and I was then able to transport it to a nearby park to let it go. Once it was back in the woods, I didn't think too much else about it.

If you understand a little bit about First Aid, you know that in the aftermath of receiving a wound, you're supposed to periodically change the dressing, a band-aid in this case, until the wound has closed up enough that there is no longer a danger of infection. This bite had minimal aftermath impact upon me; or so I thought. As the days turned into weeks following my unexpected encounter complete with a totally surprising bite, I noticed that my wound seemed to be taking a long time to heal. One week went by, and so did another, and my wrist (the place the snake had left evidence of the fact that it was indeed a predator) still had not healed.

One morning I woke up early, and thoughts came to my mind about the fact that my bite still had not healed. It had been three weeks to the day since I had been bitten, and by now I was a little concerned. I started to change the dressing again, but this time I ran my finger across the wound. To my amazement, I felt something sticking "out" of my wound. Startled, I ran my finger across the wound a second time. Was I really feeling what I thought I felt? I lifted my wrist to a position in front of some intense light, and I clearly saw what the problem was. There was a tooth, not a fang, sticking out of my wrist! I quickly located a pair of tweezers, and gently removed the tooth. I ran my finger across the wound again, and I felt a second tooth sticking out. Tweezers were again brought to bear. I ran my finger across the wound a third time and felt another tooth! That one was removed as well. So, that little snake had left three of his razor-sharp, rodent-catching "pieces" of killing equipment sticking out of my wrist for three weeks.

Well, that was it for me! I decided that day that I was done with snakes. I didn't want to learn about them anymore. I didn't want to handle them anymore. And I certainly didn't want to get bitten anymore. That one bite did me in, and it was the last one for me. That was in 2015, and to this day I have never physically "handled" another snake. (I still have to address the spiritual ones, as we all do in this life.) But please don't misconstrue my decision in the wrong way. Just because I decided that I was done, and decided that I didn't want to handle snakes anymore, does not automatically mean that there was not still a heart-level connection to these creatures that I had been obsessed with for what seemed like all my life. The heart stronghold of the Serpent was still there. And that thing (the attachment) would speak to me every now and then to try to draw me back into its' slavery. On the inside, I was still captive. Now we come to another critically important point. This point is another earmark of obsessive behavior.

In your life (and in mine), when you identify, and openly look at what justifiably may be called "problem" areas in your life, whatever situations had occurred to cause the problem, or whatever "attachments" had entered to create the problem, said "things" always want to draw you back into the problem. Remember, we're talking about "spiritual" snakes. Whenever a true follower of the Lord Jesus Christ is "disconnected" (set free) from a device of the Serpent, the enemy is relentless in working to regain control over the man or woman. In truth, *more* "snakes" get assigned to the situation by *the* Snake, and if this intensified attack succeeds, the end result will be much, much worse. This is exactly what Jesus was talking about in the Book of Matthew…

> *"When an unclean spirit goes out of a man, he goes through dry places, seeking rest, and finds none. "Then he says, 'I will return to my house from which I came.' And when he comes he finds it empty, swept, and put in order. "Then he goes out and takes with him seven other spirits more wicked than himself, and they enter and dwell there; and the last state of that man is worse than the first. So shall it also be with this wicked generation."*
> Matthew 12:43-44

Do you see the point in what we are talking about? Yes, I had made a decision, and it was the right decision. But my heart was still somewhat "all in", to a certain extent, and that is where the battle was being waged. The question you as the reader should be asking is this, "How does one get the heart disconnected from the obsession (the snakes)?" Does Jesus have the answer to this deeply rooted issue? The answer to that last question is a resounding "Yes!", and I can personally testify to this great truth. More than that, I am quite unashamedly willing to do so, for all who are willing to hear. The answer is found in the Ministry of Jesus.

Let's bring back before our eyes the relevant scripture passage purposely listed at the beginning of this book on the Dedication page. Here it is again:

"The Spirit of the LORD is upon Me,
Because He has anointed Me to
Preach the gospel to the poor;
He has sent Me to heal the brokenhearted,
To proclaim liberty to the captives
And recovery of sight to the blind,
To set at liberty those who are oppressed;
To proclaim the acceptable year of the LORD."
Luke 4:18-19

If, despite your best efforts, you find that your heart is still connected or engaged with behavior that you no longer want to pursue, you must understand that you are still a "captive" of it on some level. You are also still being "oppressed" by it. There is still a "stronghold" of the enemy in your life evidenced by the fact that your heart is still connected. The good news is that you can truly be free of it on every level. All the aspects of the Ministry of Jesus are still operational in the earth today, however, sometimes it's a journey to get to the place where certain blessings of His Ministry can be released into your life. My journey led me to Waco, Texas. There I was blessed to find a ministry that focuses on the aspect of the Ministry of Jesus which truly sets the captive free.

101

This particular ministry of Jesus is sometimes called a "deliverance" ministry, but don't let the enemy use a name to scare you. You do have to be very sensitive to following the leading of the Holy Spirit when seeking to be "delivered" (which simply means "set free") from a long-standing connection to anything that pulls you away from the perfect will of God for your life. Obviously, my obsession with snakes was one of those things. How did it work? To be honest, it was a process...

Once I began attending the regular worship services of the organization that actively conducted this type of ministry, there was an initial "get to know you" season which lasted for a few months. After my membership at this church was established, I began having in-depth conversations with the pastor about my deep, sincere desire to be totally free from the obsession we have discussed at length in this resource, as well as other "snakes" that had attached themselves to me early in my life. The church provided me with a resource to read/study regarding deliverance in preparation for this ministry. (The resource shared with me is titled, They Shall Expel Demons by Dr. Derek Prince.) I **diligently** read the information provided, then formally **requested** to receive this ministry. In May of 2015, through the intense prayers of a specially selected team of mighty prayer warriors at this church, which included the pastor, I was finally set free from my lifelong heart-felt infatuation with snakes. The connection that occurred that fateful day at the London Zoo was severed, and I have never had a desire for catching or handling snakes ever again! I am forever grateful to God for His direction of that pastor, and his effective team of prayer warriors, as they were the liberating Hand of God in my life through the

Ministry of Jesus. So, the truth shared with you earlier most assuredly bears repeating again here at the end...

"Therefore if the Son makes you free,
you shall be free indeed."
John 8:36

Author Note:

While this is the end of my journey writing this resource, for now, it may not be the end of the journey for you. You may find that you have developed an inquisitiveness, a longing, or a desire to learn more about the spiritual truths shared in this unique resource. That's good! You may even call it a thirst or hunger for more real truth in an unreal (fallen) world. Having an insatiable thirst for truth is one of the most valuable qualities that a person can have. It is one of the "earmarks" of a person that has a "royal" spirit (heart). If this describes you, then please read and carefully consider the radical life-changing pages that follow the Recapitulation in the Epilogue. For it contains **The Message** of this book.

"It is the glory of God to conceal a matter,
But the glory of kings is to
search out a matter."
Proverbs 25:2

Epilogue

EP'ILOGUE, *noun* ep'ilog. [Latin epilogus, from Gr. conclusion; to conclude; to speak.]

1. In oratory, a conclusion; the closing part of a discourse, in which <u>the principal matters are **recapitulated**</u>.

2. In the drama, a speech or short poem addressed to the spectators by one of the actors, <u>after the conclusion</u> of the play.

(Emphasis added.)

Recapitulation

The Introduction of this resource begins with eight very interesting questions focusing on behaviors related to infatuations and obsessions. While I, as the author, draw on some of my own real-world experiences regarding my former infatuation-turned-obsession where snakes are concerned, the real Message of this book is critically more important than my individual experiences. The concept of "spiritual snakes" which cannot be seen with our physical eyes is also introduced. It also touches on the revealed mission statement of hell, and how our own ignorance about how the enemy of our souls operates can lead to our own destruction as well as others close to us.

Chapter One chronicles the specifics of how my infatuation with snakes first began. It clearly portrays a number of viable alternatives on which I could have focused my life during my childhood other than snakes. What occurred to me that cataclysmic day at the London Zoo can easily be described as "mind-warping", to the extent that all things snakes completely dominated my thinking from that day on. My interest in more knowledge about snakes was insatiable, leading me to read nearly every book about snakes that I could get my hands on for years to come. Although my dramatic encounter with the Serpent in the snake house certainly makes interesting reading, the initiation of most infatuations is probably much less monumental.

By the time my family moved back from England in 1973 (Chapter 2), the knowledge I had multiplied in my head regarding snakes, was looking for opportunities for real-world encounters. If you are the parent or guardian of a child with an obviously recognizable infatuation (there are signs), you might consider whether it might evolve into a long-term obsession. Also, parental suppression efforts may actually be counter-productive, resulting in strengthening the infatuation rather than negating it. If the child in question begins declaring their pursuit of their infatuation in the future as an adult, you might want to take their repeated vocalized self-declarations very seriously, because it just may come to pass. Even as children, our words have power.

After moving to the South in the summer of 1975, my infatuation-now-turned-obsession was developing a more dangerous facet, not only for myself, but also for my loved ones (Chapter 3). My obsession had morphed into a pursuit to acquire at almost any cost. Parental boundaries had lost virtually all restraint leading to the development of a willingness to pursue what I wanted even in secret. A very self-destructive and self-serving habit began to take root in my life. At this level of obsession others, like my little brother, were dragged into supporting my obsession at my insistence. The new activity of regularly attending church did nothing to stop my pursuit of snakes. In fact, this new activity tended to create more confusion rather than positive change in me. Nevertheless, seeds were sown in me, and it did help me to be open to the Word of God later in life. My introduction to volunteering at the pet shop helped galvanize my obsession, and it continued to grow.

The next military family move in 1976 to Wichita Falls, Texas, did not really provide much in the way of new herpetological experiences, much to my regret (Chapter 4). However, this is the season of my life where "spiritual" snakes began to rise up in my life, precipitated by a number of deeply depressing teenage events. The unexpected loss of a very close friend my sophomore year at Hirschi High School, was the first depressive event which had a significant demoralizing impact upon me in the spring of 1979. In the fall of that same year, the second more deadly device of the enemy exploded in my life with yet another military family move. In the middle of my junior year at Hirschi, we moved back to the South, to a place called Valdosta, Georgia. This was the hardest move of my life, and the one that absolutely wreaked havoc on my mind, will, and emotions. An inborn gift of God in the form of musical ability had much to do my restored desire to continue to move forward with my life.

However, the primary objective of Chapter Four is a deep exploration of the idea of "spiritual" snakes, which was first suggested in the Introduction. A close look at who our real enemy is (Satan), how he wars against us, and what is offered to every person at the Cross of Calvary, is the pinnacle of this resource. A list of ways that the enemy attacks us, influences our thinking, and draws us into sinful behaviors, emphasizes the many inroads that spiritual snakes (demons) can utilize to enter our lives without obviously announcing their entry, fulfilling the mission of hell, which is to steal, kill, and destroy.

Chapter Five documents the most dangerous steps yet of my obsession with snakes. After graduating from high school in Valdosta, I went to college in Troy, Alabama, to attend Troy State University. And just as I had declared for many years before then, I designated Biology as my Major in my quest to become a Herpetologist. No time was wasted in finally interacting with venomous snakes as I had longed for since I was young. Courting danger became routine as I grew increasingly comfortable with animals designed to kill. My spiritual new birth did nothing to change my pursuit of snakes, as others began to be drawn into helping fulfill what became my nightmare. My desire to seek employment as a Herpetologist won out in my senior year of college, and I dropped out to take the position at the Dallas Zoo.

I would have to say that my job as a Reptile Keeper was one of the most unusual jobs I have ever had (Chapter 6). Of course, I learned a lot more about snakes and their care during my short tenure; but I also learned a lot about people, and even more about myself. What I learned about myself was quite a surprise, to say the least, and the result was an epiphany. I had been "had" by the Serpent. Following my plan, I had realized my dream, but ultimately it turned out to be not at all what I really wanted in life. I had missed my calling. Why did I miss my calling? That is not only the question in my life, but for many others as well. The simplest answer is found in my failure to deny myself, to truly take up my cross, and follow Him when I was born again. Hanging on to my thoughts, my feelings, my desires, and my plans, left me confused, lost, and far from the perfect plan of Heaven for my life. But God...

Chapter Seven in our journey brought us (me!) finally to the place where I became disconnected from my former obsession once and for all. An unusual non-venomous snakebite, followed by an even more unusual length of time to heal; as well as the discovery of "critter" teeth left by the little predator, finally did me in. Enough was enough! The time came to decide to put away my childhood "thing". However, my decision was not enough. Ultimately, connecting with a charismatic church in Waco, Texas, is where I finally found my Freedom From Snakes! The monumental question for you, dear reader, is are you ready to be free from your snakes? The point is that in your heart of hearts Freedom From [YOUR] Snakes must be what **you** genuinely want. And that is the rest of the story...

The LORD Has A Plan

"For I know the thoughts that I think toward
you,says the LORD, thoughts of peace and
not of evil, to give you a future and a hope.
Then you will call upon Me and go and
pray to Me, and I will listen to you.
And you will seek Me and find Me when
you search for Me with all your heart."
Jeremiah 29:11-13

"For I know the thoughts that I think
toward you, saith the LORD,
thoughts of peace, and not of evil,
to give you an expected end."
Jeremiah 29:11 KJV

"'For I know the plans that I have for
you,' declares the LORD, 'plans for
welfare and not for calamity
to give you a future and a hope."
Jeremiah 29:11 NASV
(Emphasis added.)

A Desire For More

If you were helped in any way during the reading of this work, I praise God with you! God the Father, through the Cross of Jesus Christ, and the power of His Holy Spirit, is always trying to lead us to a better place, our best place, in Him. And I truly hope that this little resource has been utilized to that end in your life. It certainly was in mine.

I also hope that this layman's consideration of obsessive behavior has caused you to truthfully ascertain whether or not you have areas in your life that need to be addressed. Since you continued on in your journey by reading this section, there exists an operational assumption that you have discovered that you have a leading or a stirring deep on the inside to receive more spiritual direction or understanding. The pages that follow may be most helpful.

I call this content "The Conversation", and it is the great biblical account of one of the most important discussions ever held in human history. As you will see, every person alive will sooner or later be confronted with the failures and limitations of our humanity, all of which requires us to once and for all make an eternal decision. The choice is eternity with God, or eternity without God. The purpose of The Conversation is to help you decide to choose eternity with Him. And with all my heart, I truly hope that you will.

Nothing on Earth, or anywhere else in the universe for that matter, can compare with the excellency of knowing the Creator of the universe as your Heavenly Father. And after having chosen to receive His Son Jesus Christ as your personal Savior, Almighty God will become your Heavenly Father for the rest of your days. Amen!

The Message

More than a few times I have referred to the Lord Jesus as "The Message". Make no mistake about it, truly He is the Message of this book. That's why some of Names are recounted in the Front Matter of this book, that there may be no doubt. That list too, is not at all exhaustive. That's why The beautiful Lion Head graphic, again in the Front Matter, represents Him. Whether in Darryl Horn Writes resources, or on Darryl Horn Writes correspondence, on Darryl Horn Writes clothing, or on the Darryl Horn Writes website, the Lion Head is exclusively about Him. You could consider it His Signature. Why is all of this so very important? I'll give you three reasons straight from the Word of God Himself...

"And I, if I am lifted up from the earth,
will draw all peoples to Myself."
John 12:32

"Jesus said to him, 'I am the way, the truth,
and the life. No one comes to the Father
except through Me."
John 14:6

"Nor is there salvation in any other, for
there is no other name under heaven given
among men by which we must be saved."
Acts 4:12

The Conversation

One of the most piercingly important and life-changing conversations in human history is recorded for us in the 3rd Chapter of the New Testament Gospel of John. It is a poignant conversation between the Lord Jesus Himself and one of the most recognized religious leaders of His day, a man known as Nicodemus. We know that it was a very personal discussion, and it was most likely secretive, because Nicodemus met Jesus at night. It is certainly worth sharing with you in its' entirety, as many eternal and liberating truths can be drawn from this one great passage.

Over two thousand years later, the truths exposed within this great passage are still just as powerful, and just as relevant for our generation as it was for the generation living at the time Jesus physically led His earthly ministry. If at all possible, you might consider taking steps to limit any distractions around you, as these next few pages may be some of the most important pages you ever read...

1 There was a man of the Pharisees named Nicodemus, a ruler of the Jews.

2 This man came to Jesus by night and said to Him, "Rabbi, we know that You are a teacher come from God; for no one can do these signs that You do unless God is with him."

3 Jesus answered and said to him, "Most assuredly, I say to you, unless one is born again, he cannot see the kingdom of God."

4 Nicodemus said to Him, "How can one be born when he is old? Can he enter a second time into his mother's womb and be born?"

5 Jesus answered, "Most assuredly, I say to you, unless one is born of water and the Spirit, he cannot enter the kingdom of God."

6 "That which is born of the flesh is flesh, and that which is born of the Spirit is spirit."

7 "Do not marvel that I say to you, 'You must be born again.'

8 "The wind blows where it wishes, and you hear the sound of it, but cannot tell where it comes from or where it goes. So is everyone who is born of the Spirit."

9 Nicodemus answered and said to Him, "How can these things be?"

10 Jesus answered and said to him, "Are you the teacher of Israel, and do not know these things?

11 "Most assuredly, I say to you, We speak what We know and testify what We have seen, and you do not receive Our witness.

12 "If I have told you earthly things and you do not believe, how will you believe if I tell you heavenly things?

13 "No one has ascended to heaven but He who came down from heaven, *that is*, the Son of Man who is in heaven.

14 "And as Moses lifted up the serpent in the wilderness, even so must the Son of Man be lifted up,

15 "that whoever believes in Him should not perish but have eternal life.

16 "For God so loved the world that He gave His only begotten Son, that whoever believes in Him should not perish but have everlasting life.

17 "For God did not send His Son into the world to condemn the world, but that the world through Him might be saved.

18 "He who believes in Him is not condemned; but he who does not believe in Him is condemned already, because he has not believed in the name of the only begotten Son of God."

John Chapter 3, Verses 1-18

There you have it; one of the most poignant important conversations in the entire history of Mankind recorded for our benefit in these last days. It is overflowing with truth, direction, and wisdom for our lives today *if* we truly seek them. The eternal truths richly deposited in these brief verses of Scripture have the power to bring about life-enhancing changes that will forever satisfy us *if* we simply choose to receive them. God has held nothing back from us in His incredible pursuit of close relationship with those who truly desire to be His.

Now, let's see if we can draw out just a few of these jewels of truth, treasure if you will, that can be of great blessing in your life today! For the sake of simplicity, our limited examination of this passage will not go in the order of its' presentation, just so you know. So, without making this complicated in any way, here are several powerful truths we can extract from this passage that benefit us today...

Truth Number 1:

The richest and most obvious truth in this hallowed passage of Scripture, in my opinion, is found towards the end of the conversation. "For God so loved..., that He gave..." (vs. 16). The verse has "the world", but you can certainly make it personal by reading the verse out loud and substituting "me" where it says "world".

Example: "For God so loved me, Darryl, that He gave His only begotten Son that I, Darryl, who believes in Him should not perish but have everlasting life." It doesn't matter who you are, what you've done, or where you've been. If you **or I** would have been the only one that needed Him, God still would have given His Son. He gave that which is most precious to Him. He gave His Son. He gave Jesus. There is no other gift that you could ever receive that compares in any way whatsoever to the gift of Jesus. He is **the Gift** of all gifts.

Truth Number 2:

Notice that God did not send His Son to accuse, point fingers at, or condemn anyone (vs. 17). That was not what He was about. And it still isn't. He is our Salvation, not our condemnation. But please don't confuse that truth with the fact that there is coming a day when He will most assuredly execute judgement. If we wish to avoid that terrible day, the only way is found in Him.

Truth Number 3:

Verse 18 clearly tells us that our salvation, everlasting life, is in "His name", Who is "the only begotten Son of God". This verse also tells us what is required of us to activate, embrace, and receive our salvation, and that, too, is plainly made clear. It is our simple, child-like belief (faith, trust) in Him.

Truth Number 4:

Since I just mentioned belief in Him that starts out child-like (but doesn't remain there), let's reflect upon two critically important verses from the same gospel (John) just two chapters before this great conversation between Jesus and Nicodemus. This is not another record of a conversation, but truth penned by the apostle John about Jesus.

> *"But as many as received Him, to them He gave*
> *the right to become children of God,*
> *to those who believe in His name:*
> *"who were born, not of blood, nor of the*
> *will of the flesh, nor of the will*
> *of man, but of God."*
> *John 1:12-13*

Here in verse twelve, we find the powerful connection between believing (faith, trust) and receiving Him (as our Savior). Whoever believes in Him, and personally receives Him as both Lord and Savior becomes born again of the Spirit of God.

Truth Number 5:

If you would exercise your right to become a child of God, you must be born again. Only then can you begin to experience, to walk in as it were, the priceless blessings of the Kingdom of God. Belief gives us the access (right) to the kingdom as our priceless inheritance, and it can be yours today! You can begin receiving and enjoying some of your inheritance as a child of the King even before you leave planet Earth!

Truth Number 6:

The verses we have looked at thus far make it clear that Jesus was sent to our world to save us. What we haven't addressed is the "why?" Why did Jesus have to come? Why do we need Him so desperately? Why was Jesus tortured so mercilessly, and crucified on a cross? Why do we have to come to Him just as we are in our wretched condition. The answers to these questions can easily be boiled down to one remarkably simple word: sin.

It is through sin that all the evils of this world have come. Sin is the answer to the "Why?". And none of us has missed out in this area, no not one. Do you remember that brief list of negative behaviors and qualities on pages 66-68? Every single thing listed probably involves sin and must be dealt with according to the Word of God. And by the way, without diving into any deep theological definitions of this commonly misunderstood word; to sin simply means to miss the mark. God has a perfect plan for dealing with sin, and it is called repentance. Repentance always comes before salvation, and there is absolutely no way around it. So, what is biblical repentance? Let's take a look…

Make Much of Repentance.

Let's start this critically important section with three penetrating questions. First, why did the Holy Spirit lead me to include this particular section leading up to the what is the most important decision a person can make in this life? Is the purpose to make it more difficult for you to enter your inheritance as a child of the King, as so many highly religious zealots have done for millennia? Could it be that many religious organizations in America make salvation so easy and profitable that they do an evil disservice to both the lost and the Savior Himself? Make no mistake about it, repentance is the key that opens your door to salvation. Then once you are truly saved, your spiritual crucifixion is what makes it work.

> '"Truly, these times of ignorance God overlooked, but <u>now commands all men everywhere</u> to repent,..."'
> ### Acts 17:30
> *(Emphasis added.)*

Surely after having just read the above verse, there can be no ambiguity regarding the necessity of repentance. That's why the emphasis (underline) was added to the Scripture. It's not a good idea. It's not a request. It's not a suggestion. It's not what so-and-so told you. The opinion of any man or woman us not a factor at all. For our own good, every single one of us, it is a command. And there is absolutely no way around it. In fact, the Lord Jesus made this truth crystal clear (twice!) in Luke's Gospel saying as follows...

"…[U]nless you repent you will all likewise perish."
Luke 13:3, 5

The Lord Jesus does not mince any words there. So, we're not going to mince any words in this resource. Consequently, why is repentance commanded by God, and why Jesus say that we will perish without it? Do we *really* need to examine what He meant by "perish"? As far as this work is concerned, not so much. While we will not explore what perish means right here, I will say that it really does not sound good…

"For godly sorrow produces repentance leading to salvation…"
2 Corinthians 7:10a

As you can see, repentance is unequivocally necessary before we receive our salvation. The product of repentance that is produced from heartfelt godly sorrow for all our sins is not a negative thing in any way. It's all good! It produces what we desperately need and deeply desire in our heart of hearts. When you truly repent, you can't lose.

Repentance is way more than the shallow general apology for all the "mistakes" (sins) of our past. That is simply a cowardly acknowledge that, agree, or disagree if you must; but it is reprehensibly repugnant to a Holy God. True repentance is a multifaceted jewel in the Eyes of the King of Creation, and it encompasses way more than many "churches" in modern America would lead people to believe. It is a deeply heartfelt sorrow rooted in the recognition that our sins, both yours and mine, necessitated the Son of God to relinquish His eternal position in Heaven, for a season, to be miraculously born on Earth by the Holy Spirit, to live a perfect sinless life, ultimately to be crucified on a cross, to save each one of us from our sins. He gave His best, His all, and He deserves no less from us. Repentance is definitely not the place to cut corners. That will never work.

"The Lord is not slack concerning His promise, as some count slackness, but is longsuffering toward us, not willing that any should perish but that all should come to repentance."
2 Peter 3:9

Hopefully no one reading resource is in the position of "pushing back" against the Holy Spirit regarding the absolute necessity of repentance. If so…

"…because He has appointed a day on which He will judge the world in righteousness by the Man whom He has ordained. He has given assurance of this to all by raising Him from the dead."'
Acts 17:31

Therefore, I strongly encourage you to make much of your repentance. You will never regret it, and without it, you too, most assuredly, will perish.

The Plan of Salvation

*"For all have sinned and fall short
of the glory of God."*
<u>*Romans 3:23*</u>
*"For the wages of sin is death, but
the gift of God is eternal life in
Jesus Christ our Lord."*
<u>*Romans 6:23*</u>
*"But God demonstrates His own love
toward us, in that while we were
still sinners, Christ died for us."*
<u>*Romans 5:8*</u>

*"…that if you confess with your mouth
the Lord Jesus and believe in
your heart that God has raised Him
from the dead, you will be saved."*
<u>*Romans 10:9*</u>
*"For with the heart one believes unto
righteousness, and with the mouth
confession is made unto salvation."*
<u>*Romans 10:10*</u>
*"For 'whoever calls on the name
of the LORD shall be saved.'"*
<u>*Romans 10:13*</u>

123

The Key To The Journey

The thoughts shared in this box are arguably the most important that I am compelled to share **before** you take your very first step in establishing the God of heaven and earth as your Heavenly Father. The point that has to be emphasized is that this step is critical to the success of your walk with Him. Its importance cannot be overstated because it is the only thing that works. What is this key? Very simply, it is dying to yourself. If you are going to follow Jesus, dying to yourself is **not** optional. It is a sometimes excruciatingly painful lifelong **process**. The Lord Jesus said it this way…

> *"… 'Whoever desires to come after Me, let him deny himself, and take up his cross, and follow Me.'"*
> *Mark 8:34*

So important is it to start with this process, that it is specifically addressed in the new birth prayer for salvation on the next page. You may not understand the whole process when you start your journey (no one does!), but you do have to be willing to participate in the process by faith. If you are not willing to participate in your own spiritual crucifixion, you might seriously reconsider taking the next step. The only way to start a new life is to die to the old one. If you truly want a new beginning in Christ, turn the page, and follow the instructions from your heart.

Prayer to Receive Christ as
Your Lord & Savior

The very first step in establishing a personal, life-sustaining, eternal relationship with God, is to say out loud (confess) **from your heart**, a very simple prayer...

Lord Jesus,

I humbly come before You to voice my **confession** of faith in You. I truly **believe** that You are the Son of God, and that He raised You from the dead. I **confess** that I am a **sinner**; that many times I have missed the mark in the sinful choices I have made; and that because of my choices I deserve to be separated eternally from God. However, today I fully **repent** of all my sins...; and I **ask** You to forgive me, and cleanse me with Your precious **Blood**. I ask You to clothe me with Your righteousness by faith.

As I take this first step in becoming a child of God, I fully commit myself to deny myself, and take up my cross, and follow You. I receive You as my Lord and Savior, and I give You my **heart**, my life, and all that I am, **asking** You to mold me and shape into a vessel of honor for Your Glory in these last days. Thank You for loving me and saving me. Thank You for adding me to God's family of believers, the **Church**, which is Your Body. Thank You for my new life in You. In Your Name, Amen!

If you have prayed that prayer aloud in its entirety, and truly meant it from your heart, I want you to know that right this moment there is a thunderous celebration happening in Heaven because of the exercise of *your* faith in *your* new birth! You have a wonderful inheritance in Him, and it is now truly accessible to you in Him. Praise the Lord!

Growing Up in Christ

Congratulations on your heartfelt declaration of faith! Your new beginning begins like every other new believer from the birth of the Church in Acts Chapter One. Everyone is born again as a new baby in Christ. One of the first instructions He gives every one of us is found in the New Testament Book of First Peter.

> *"...as newborn babes, desire the pure milk of the word, that you may grow thereby..."*
> 1 Peter 2:2

Therefore, one of the first tools necessary for your new life in Christ that is absolutely a must-have, is your personal copy of the Word of God. Simply called the Bible, the word itself is looked at by some, including me, as a very clever easy-to-remember acronym...

(**B**asic **I**nstructions **B**efore **L**eaving **E**arth)

Yes, there are many, many Bibles available, thanks to first the printing press, then the modern Internet, but not all of them are worthy building your new life upon. Especially as a new babe in Christ, you should avoid translations that are the product of one person. That is a most dangerous road to travel, my friend. Additionally, it would behoove you to utilize a time-tested translation such as the great King James Version (KJV), or the New King James Version (NKJV), as your go-to resource to build the foundation of your new faith in Christ. Either of these translations will be most beneficial for you. Also, one that has the words of Christ in red, called

126

a Red-Letter Edition is also highly recommended. So, let confidently recommend the Bible that has significantly impacted many true followers of Jesus Christ, especially me, and that I have found to be both to highly respected, and very, very trustworthy. It is called the <u>Spirit Filled Life Bible</u>, it is the primary resource of the vastly overwhelming biblical passages shared in this resource, and you can find the catalogue information for it on the copyright page of this work (in the front matter).

"All Scripture is given by inspiration of God,
and is profitable for doctrine,
for reproof, for correction,
for instruction in righteousness,
that the man of God may be complete,
thoroughly equipped for every good work."
2 Timothy 3:16,17

"Let the word of Christ dwell in you
richly in all wisdom..."
Col. 3:16a

"Blessed is the man Who walks not
in the counsel of the ungodly,
Nor stands in the path of sinners,
Nor sits in the seat of the scornful;

But his delight is in the law of the LORD,
And in His law he meditates
day and night."
Psalm 3:1-2

Now, having your own copy of the Bible is a great start, but not having a strong Spirit-led plan for personal growth is absolutely not. Of course, any of the words of Jesus in the New Testament can be powerful in your new life; you cannot go wrong there. Monumental growth can yours in the Gospel of John, some of which you have already read (Remember the Conversation?). You certainly don't want to overlook the strategic truths in the great Book of Ephesians either. Please don't miss Ephesians Chapter Six. It cannot be emphasized enough that the survival of your walk depends on it.

However, if you were to ask me what's one of my most favorite biblical plans for personal growth, I would very quickly respond with a passage of Scripture from the Book of Second Peter. So important is this plan for the lifelong growth process of all followers of the Lord Jesus, including me, it would truly be a travesty not to reproduce the entire passage from the first chapter...

"3 ...as His divine power has given to us
all things that pertain to
life and godliness, through the
knowledge of Him who called us
by glory and virtue,
4 by which have been given to us
exceedingly great and precious promises,
that through these
you may be partakers of
the divine nature, having escaped the
corruption that is in the world through lust.
5 But also for this very reason,
giving all diligence, add to
your faith virtue, to virtue knowledge,
6 to knowledge self-control,
to self a control perseverance,
to perseverance godliness,
7 to godliness brotherly kindness,
and to brotherly kindness love."

"8 For if these things are yours and abound,
you will neither be barren nor
unfruitful in the knowledge
of our Lord Jesus Christ.
9 For he who lacks these things
is short-sighted, even to blindness,
and has forgotten that he
was cleansed from his old sins.
10 Therefore, brethren, be even more
diligent to make your call
and election sure, for if
you do these things you
will never stumble;
11 for so an entrance will be supplied
to you abundantly into the
everlasting kingdom of
our Lord and Savior
Jesus Christ."

2 Peter 1: 3-12

The reason so many Scriptures have been included about the Word is so that you may clearly see and appreciate all it has to offer us in Christ. Your spiritual inheritance in Him cannot be received without the Light with which it guides our steps. And there is no way on earth that we can be strong in God without His Word in these last days.

So, let me share with you one last thing before I close out this resource. Let me close with one last awesome promise of the King of the Universe from the great New Testament Book of Romans…

"What shall we say to these things?
If God is for us, who can
be against us?"
<u>*Romans 8:31*</u>

To which I just can't help but say,

"Praise the Lord!"

Darryl T. Horn

"Finally, my brethren, be strong in the Lord
and in the power of His might.
Put on the whole armor of God, that you
may be able to stand against the wiles of the devil.
For we do not wrestle against flesh and blood,
but against principalities, against powers,
against the rulers of the darkness of this age,
against spiritual hosts of wickedness
in the heavenly places.
Therefore take up the whole armor of God,
that you may be able to withstand
in the evil day, and having done all,
to stand. Stand therefore,
having girded your waist with truth,
having put on the breastplate of righteousness,
and having shod your feet with the
preparation of the gospel of peace;
above all, taking the shield of faith with
which you will be able to quench
all the fiery darts of the wicked one.
And take the helmet of salvation,
and the sword of the Spirit, which
is the word of God; praying with
all prayer and supplication in the Spirit,
being watchful to this end with all perseverance
and supplication for all the saint…"
Ephesians 6:10-18

Appendices

A Few Selected Thoughts on
Herpetology & Snakes

As is mentioned in the first chapter, Herpetology is that branch of the Biological Sciences that deal with the study of reptiles and amphibians. Included in these overly broad terms are lizards, turtles, alligators, crocodiles, frogs, toads, salamanders, and, of course, snakes. What I have just shared is a general overview, and if this were an actual biological course on Herpetology, my overview would contain a few more details than I have included here. But since the door to the "presence" of the Serpent in my life has been closed now for some seven years, I have chosen not to re-open said door by going back to study anything regarding my former obsession with snakes for the writing of this book. The only exception is a distant observation of the deterioration in the video-recorded **<u>foolish</u>** handling of venomous snakes widely displayed on social media nowadays.

Therefore, if you have found that there are a few discrepancies in specifics that I have written regarding snakes, such as the Latin names identified, or other details I may have overlooked, you will just have to forgive me. It was not intentional. I have not kept up with changes in nomenclature over these last two or three decades, and I no longer have any interest in learning the latest herpetological nomenclature again. I have truly been delivered, and I thank God Almighty for the Ministry of Jesus Christ in my life which has set me free! I am no longer a slave.

Now, regarding the fear of snakes, which was also mentioned in Chapter 1, I believe that it is commonly known that fears are many times referred to as "phobias". If you were to search online, I am sure you could find a long list of different types of phobias. There have been movies based on some phobias, such as those made about the fear of spiders. The fear of spiders is called Arachnophobia (I confess - I did look that one up!). I have never been "into" spiders, I have no regrets about it, and I am not ashamed! Anyhow, the fear of snakes is called Ophidiophobia. I have always found the origin (or naming) of this particular phobia most interesting. One of my favorite snakes back in the day, which I had always wanted to "handle", was a King Cobra. I learned early in my life that at over eighteen feet long, the gargantuan King Cobra was listed at one time in the Guinness (Book) of World Records as the longest venomous snake in the world. Once I learned that fact, I was "drawn" to it. And as snakes go, it truly is one impressive snake.

An adult King Cobra possesses enough venom at one time to kill at least ten adult human beings or more. It has no qualms about standing its' ground, and if you were ever to happen across one unexpectedly, you would have a real problem. Cobras can lift about a third of their body off the ground. That means that a fifteen-foot King Cobra can "stand up" to a height of four or five feet off the ground. For a lot of peoples, that sight at close range would not only be terrifying, but it could also be somewhat paralyzing as well. And that is unfortunate, because the act of this Cobra "standing up" is a clear indicator that it feels threatened, and if you can, it is way past time for you to quickly disappear. If you don't, then here comes the bite. And it's not just any bite either. A bite from this serpent, if venom is injected, is immediately life-threatening.

You see, the venom of a King Cobra is an enormously powerful neurotoxin. Without boring you with too much detail, it means that the venom acts on your nervous system. Within a short few minutes, you will begin to feel the effects. Your heart will begin racing (if it wasn't already from fear), your breathing will begin to become difficult, and organ systems will soon be affected as well. News flash! None of this is good for you. And yet, I wanted to "handle" them. Remember in Chapter 2 where I said something about my not having a firm grasp on reality? There you go! I truly did not have a firm grasp on reality. I'm trying to tell that this snake can kill you dead, and I "wanted" to voluntarily get close enough to it to handle it? How idiotic! (I'm talking about myself!) If you see one of these critters outside of an enclosure, it's time for you to make **your** Olympic trial run too, but in the opposite direction. This is not a game.

Anyway, I said all of that to say that Ophidiophobia, the fear of snakes, comes from the scientific name of the King Cobra. The scientific name is _Ophiophagus hannah_. Do you see the connection? ("Ophidio" is drawn out of "Ophio".) If you are still having difficulty in this area, please accept my apologies. I no longer consider myself a herpetologist, and you stand a better chance of getting a good understanding about this by contacting a currently embedded professional, if that's what you want. But now you know more than the average person about the origin of Ophidiophobia, and if you are ever asked that question on a game show, you'll win! Just don't get bitten by one.

Speaking of the "bite", I mentioned something earlier called a "dry bite". Just because a person is bitten by a venomous snake, does not automatically mean that venom was injected. (If you are going to err, please err on the side of caution.) Some snakes have been found to have the capability of biting without injecting venom. If you were to conduct an anatomical examination of the inside of a venomous snakes' head, such as a rattlesnake, you would find that there are muscles around the venom "sacks" which squeeze out the venom when the snake bites. This hypothesis regarding dry bites is exceedingly difficult to verify because to confirm this theory you have to utilize "live" venomous snakes that bite at your convenience and not theirs. How would you "measure" whether the venom sacks did or did not activate? This type of study, to say the least, would be a little bit prickly. See Appendix 2 for more information regarding dry bites from a medical professional.

I certainly could go on and on about many different topics related to my former obsession with snakes. Thankfully, there is a principle called, "Use it or lose it", and this certainly applies to my pursuit of knowledge and experience with snakes. I no longer handle snakes and have no desire to do so. And I no longer enjoy talking about snakes either like I did in the past. If you were ever to attempt to engage me in a discussion about them, if I do not respond, please don't feel hurt, ignored, or offended. The only significantly worthwhile reason now for discussing snakes, as far as I am concerned, is when the discussion revolves around how to eradicate "spiritual" snakes.

Isn't it interesting how most people are so eager to kill physical snakes, but give no thought(s), or take no action regarding the spiritual "snakes" which are clearly evident in their lives? It is our heritage as the children of God to "tread", or "trample" as it were, on snakes and scorpions as instructed in Luke 10:19. How about we end this appendix with that great passage of scripture?

"Behold, I give you the authority to trample on serpents and scorpions, and over all the power of the enemy, and nothing by any means shall hurt you."
Luke 10:19

Appendix 2

Wise As Serpents?

In the first chapter of this resource there is a reference made to a statement that Jesus said in the Book of Matthew. Here is that statement...

> *"Behold, I send you out as sheep*
> *in the midst of wolves.*
> *Therefore be wise as serpents*
> *and harmless as doves."*
> *Matthew 10:16*

I must confess that this statement puzzled me for a long time. Even after I was employed professionally as a Reptile Keeper at the Dallas Zoo, I still couldn't figure it out. I'm not sure when the Holy Spirit finally revealed to me what this passage meant, but I want to share with you my insight of the phrase "wise as serpents" from the position of a former Herpetologist. Admittedly, having some anatomical understanding of snakes is necessary, so here goes...

One of the most unique aspects about snakes is that these animals do not have eyelids. Nearly all other land habitat animals have eyelids, but snakes do not. Even their closest "relatives", lizards, have eyelids, but not the lowly snake. All of which leads to a very interesting question: How can you tell if a snake is asleep? I hate to break this news to you, but you can't! Just because it's not moving, does not necessarily mean that it's asleep. Many snakes are what is called "ambush" predators. That means these particular carnivores employ the "sit and wait" tactic of hunting for their prey.

One of the best representatives of "herps" that use this tactic is the Gaboon Viper (*Bitis gabonica*) of Africa. Did I say that the last time I checked, it was still listed in the Guinness (Book) of World Records as the snake with the longest fangs? The last Guinness listing I saw recorded fangs measuring two inches long! Just so you know, they do not make good pets, so don't even think about it. When I say these snakes are deadly, you don't even understand. We had some at the Dallas Zoo, so I have actually "handled" them, but let me tell you, my heart rate went up every time I was in proximity to one because this animal is truly lethal.

Here is an excerpt that I ran across in a book called <u>A Doctor's Devotion, A Passion for Serving</u>, written by Dr. Harry Holwerda. Among the many accomplishments of his distinguished career, Dr. Holwerda served the Lord and his profession in medical missions in Africa.

"The Gaboon Viper is the largest of the poisonous snakes and injects the most venom. Its fangs are nearly 2-1/2 inches in length. Because of the deep injection of its venom, amputation of the bitten extremity is recommended for survival.

"In a United States Navy study, reported while I was in the military during the Vietnam War, we were given the following information: In a poisonous snake bite only 50 percent of the time is venom injected. When venom is injected, only 25 percent of the time is the dose lethal."

Quotes Used by Permission of the Author
<u>A Doctor's Devotion: A
Passion for Serving</u>
2019 Harry Holwerda
ISBN-13: 978-1-5456-8075-9
Xulon Press

Anyway, the point is this: whether a snake is awake or asleep, its' eyes are always open. So, to think you're going to "sneak up" on a snake is an exercise in idiocy. They are masters at stealth, and they always appear to be aware of their environment. Even if they happen to be asleep, and even though they have no hearing apparatus, snakes are always in tune with their environment. If one is asleep, vibrations of approaching predators or prey through sensations carried by the ground are easily picked up, and the snake starts to wake up. They do not want to miss a meal, and they probably don't want to be one either.

So, what is the wisdom from this passage? Answer: It has everything to do with spiritual awareness; being in tune to what's happing in the spiritual realm all around us. The enemy isn't sitting around taking a break to watch a football game. Remember what his game is? He exists to steal, kill, and destroy (John 10:10). It can be argued with significant intensity that his greatest weapon is our own complacency and ignorance. An environment of ignorance (which is spiritual darkness), affords him a monumental advantage to conduct his warfare against us. Not knowing is one thing. Complacency, not caring, is much, much worse.

Now, in these last days, it is not the time to be ignorant about the things of God. I'm quite sure that the place of complacency or ignorance is not where you want to be, otherwise you wouldn't be reading this book. Living a life of ignorance will never be blessed. To be ignorant is to set our own selves up to be destroyed. As children of God, we are all instructed by the Bible to *study the Word of God. To study it is way, way beyond just reading it. The rich truths of the Word of God are not usually found on the surface. It takes deep desire. It takes long-term diligence. It takes relentless effort. All of which translates into "work". But don't let that scare you. This activity is never boring, nor does it have to be an exercise conducted in drudgery. It truly is exciting and rewarding! Work in the Word of God benefits the "workman" in the here and now, as well as preparing us for eternity. I would suggest that you scrounge up some paper and something to write with. Some highlighters would be very helpful as well. Take on the humble mindset of a student. Ask the Holy Spirit to help you by guiding you into the truths of His Word.

> *"Study to shew thyself approved unto God, a workman that needeth not to be ashamed, rightly dividing the word of truth."*
> *2 Timothy 2:15 KJV*

Moses Lifted Up a Serpent?

In the Gospel of John Chapter 3, the Lord Jesus makes a very interesting statement. It is quoted in the great Scripture passage referenced on page 116, and is printed again in this appendix for our focus...

> *"And as Moses lifted up the serpent in*
> *the wilderness, even so must the*
> *Son of Man be lifted up,*
> *"that whoever believes in Him*
> *should not perish*
> *but have eternal life."*
> *John 3:14, 15*

This very interesting statement is, of course, a prophetic declaration of Jesus foretelling His crucifixion, and has its' roots in multiple Scriptures in the Old Testament. It is beyond the scope of this resource to do an exhaustive study of this critically important biblical theme, but something must be said pre-emptively to address an obvious question that many would have to be wondering. Why did Jehovah choose the image of a serpent (snake) to be the visual focus for the children of Israel to be saved after being bitten by venomous ("fiery") snakes, especially since those snakes were sent by God Himself as punishment for their rebellion? While the species of the snakes is not identified, the bite of these snakes was probably agonizingly painful, paralyzing in effect, and resulting in the demise of the one bitten.

I encourage you to read the biblical account for yourself as a primer before we address the answer to this question. It is found in the Pentateuch, the first five books of the Bible, as attributed to be written by Moses. The passage can be found in Numbers 21:4-9. For our purposes, we will limit our focus to the following verses:

> *"6 "So the LORD sent fiery serpents among*
> *the people, and they bit the people;*
> *and many of the people died.*
> *7 "…So Moses prayed for the people.*
> *8 "Then the LORD said to Moses, 'Make a*
> *fiery serpent, and set it on a pole;*
> *and it shall be that everyone who is bitten,*
> *when he looks at, shall live.'*
> *9 "So Moses made a bronze serpent, and put*
> *it on a pole; and so it was, if a serpent*
> *had bitten anyone, when he looked*
> *at the bronze serpent, he lived."*
> *Numbers 21:6-9*

So, what is our take-away from this passage? Twice in this passage we see that when a person was bitten by a "fiery" serpent (snake), when he (or she – the Scriptures do not say women, or children for that matter, were exempt) looked at the bronze serpent pole, he lived. And just so you know, "lived" means saved. They were saved from a sure death when they looked to the raised bronze serpent. We know from the 3rd chapter of Genesis that God clearly pronounced an eternal curse on the serpent in the Garden of

Eden. But again, why would God use that which He had obviously cursed, the serpent, as the only focal point for the salvation of His people in the wilderness? The answer to this question has everything to do with the following verse...

"If a man has committed a sin deserving of death, and he is put to death, and you <u>hang him on a tree</u>, His body shall not remain overnight <u>on the tree</u>, but you shall surely bury him that day, so that you do not defile the land which the LORD your God is giving you as an inheritance; for <u>he who is hanged is accursed of God</u>."
Deuteronomy 21:22-23
(Emphasis added.)

It should be clearly obvious that the above verses are specifically addressing a particular type of punishment, that of death on a tree - crucifixion. Anyone who was put to death by this method, the Bible says is "accursed". To help us drive this point home, so to speak, let's drive this point home with a couple of verses from the New Testament.

"Christ has redeemed us from the curse of the law, having become a curse for us (for it is written, '<u>Cursed is everyone who hangs on a tree</u>'),..."
Galatians 3:13
(Emphasis added.)

145

"…who Himself bore our sins in His own body
on the tree, that we, having died to sins,
might live for righteousness – by whose
stripes you were healed."
1 Peter 2:24
(Emphasis added.)

Hopefully you can see the singular inescapable truth that death by crucifixion is what are focusing on, and anyone who was put to death that way was under a curse. The laws of the Old Testament, more than six hundred, clearly say what the God of heaven and earth declares as sin. Much of the list in Chapter Four (pages 66-68) are drawn from those laws, ordinances, and prohibitions. The Lord Jesus Christ, as the visible representation of the invisible God, demonstrated by His perfect example the embodiment and fulfillment of the law during His life and ministry on Earth. This is both significant and relevant in our generation because of this next Scripture…

"Jesus Christ the same yesterday,
today, and forever."
Hebrews 13:8
(Emphasis added.)

The unchanging nature of God is an inarguable reality of the entire Bible and is worthy of more attention than can be given in this resource. But must be mentioned as we finally bring to a close this very brief examination of why Moses was directed to lift up an image of a serpent. But to be fair, let me mention one last Scripture before we, at last, answer this fairly important question.

"For I am the LORD,
I change not…"
Malachi 3:6

Starting from the curse on the serpent pronounced by God Himself in the Book of Genesis, to that which was cursed being lifted up by Moses, so those who were bitten by the serpents in the wilderness lived (were saved) when they looked at the cursed image, to the curse pronounced on anyone who was hanged (crucified) on a tree, to Jesus Himself declaring that when He would be "lifted up" (crucified) the curse on all the descendants of Adam would be born in His Body by Him. God's people in the wilderness had to look to that which is cursed to be saved. And so it is with God's people since the crucifixion and resurrection of Christ for the last two thousand plus years, and then some.

God's people had to look at that which was cursed to be saved in the wilderness. Similarly, God's people today have to look at that which was cursed to be saved. But there is way more to our salvation than looking *to* the Cross. Salvation requires us to go *through* the Cross. Denying ourselves and going through the painful process of spiritually dying to our desires, our plans, our thoughts, and our will, by taking up our own spiritual cross, is the only way that we can fully and truly follow Jesus and become one of His disciples in these last days. There is no other way. And that's why it was critically important to add the spiritual truths in the Epilogue. Take a deep look at your own life, letting the Holy Spirit guide you, and if your life does not truly reflect your spiritual crucifixion, do not rest until does. Amen!

Definitions on pages 25, 43, and 105 included by permission from the following resource:

R. Slater, Rosalie June. "Noah Webster: Founding Father of Scholarship and Education," in Noah Webster's An American Dictionary of the English Language, Facsimile First Edition. Chesapeake, Virginia: Foundation for American Christian Education, 1967.

About The Author

Called to write resources that help, teach, and give hope to other true followers of the Lord Jesus Christ in these last days, new Indie author Darryl T. Horn has just released his first book "Freedom From Snakes!". Even though he began pursuing writing in 2014, with the release of this first book, he is just now beginning to walk in the fullness of his God-given calling. Recently "called out" as a wordsmith, he already has several other works already "in process", and new Christ-centered resources are expected to be released in 2022 (Lord willing!). For more information, please visit his Author Page on Amazon (click "Follow" to receive automated updates), or go to his website:

www.darrylhornwrites.com

2 Timothy Chapter 3

1 But know this, that in the last days
perilous times will come:
2 For men will lovers of themselves,
lovers of money, boasters, proud, blasphemers,
disobedient to parents, unthankful, unholy,
3 unloving, unforgiving, slanderous,
without self-control, brutal, despisers of good,
4 traitors, headstrong, haughty, lovers of
pleasure rather than lovers of God,
5 having a form of godliness
but denying its power.
And from such people turn away.
6 For of this sort are those who creep into
households and make captives of gullible
women loaded down with sins,
led away by various lusts,
7 always learning and never able
to come to the knowledge of the truth.
8 Now as Jannes and Jambres resisted Moses,
so do these also resist the truth:
men of corrupt minds,
disapproved concerning the faith;
9 but will progress no further, for their folly
will be manifest to all, as theirs was.

10 But you have carefully followed my doctrine,
manner of life, purpose, faith,
long-suffering, love, perseverance,
11 persecutions, afflictions, which happened
to me at Antioch, at Iconium, at Lystra,
- what persecutions I endured. And out
of them all the Lord delivered me.
12 Yes, and all who desire to live godly in
Christ Jesus will suffer persecution.
13 But evil men and imposters will grow worse
and worse, deceiving and being deceived.
14 But you must continue in the things which
you have learned and been assured of,
knowing from whom you have learned them,
15 and that from childhood you have known
the Holy Scriptures, which are able
to make you wise for salvation
through faith which is in Christ Jesus.
16 All Scripture is given by inspiration of God,
and is profitable for doctrine, for reproof, for
correction, for instruction in righteousness,
17 that the man of God may be complete,
thoroughly equipped for every good work.
2Timothy 3:1-17

Made in the USA
Middletown, DE
02 March 2022